The

UGLY
TRUTH

about

MANAGING
PEOPLE

Must-Get-Right

50 MANAGEMENT CHALLENGES…
And How to Really Handle Them

Ruth King

SOURCEBOOKS, INC.
NAPERVILLE, ILLINOIS

Published by Sourcebooks, Inc.
P.O. Box 4410, Naperville, Illinois 60567-4410
(630) 961-3900
Fax: (630) 961-2168
www.sourcebooks.com

Library of Congress Cataloging-in-Publication Data

King, Ruth.
  The ugly truth about managing people : fifty (must-get-
right) management challenges and how to really handle
them / Ruth King.
       p. cm.
  Includes index.
  ISBN 978-1-4022-0913-0 (trade pbk.)
  1. Small business--Management--Handbooks, manuals,
etc. I. Title.

HD62.7.K567 2007
658.3--dc22

                                        2007019689

Printed and bound in the United States of America.
        VP 10 9 8 7 6 5 4 3 2 1

DEDICATION

This book is dedicated to the millions of managers and aspiring managers out there. I hope the stories you read on the following pages give you examples of how to manage, how not to manage, and how to succeed in your career.

CONTENTS

Foreword xiii

Introduction 1

Chapter One: Why We Are Managers 5

Part One: Fifty Stories of The Ugly Truth about Managing People

1. I Was Thrown into Management
   Lea Strickland..11
2. A Woman Sexually Harassed Me
   Anonymous...16
3. I Cursed at My Boss
   Anonymous...20
4. We Needed a Clear Pet Policy
   Richard Woods 24
5. I Managed Childish People
   Mark Miller 27
6. I Instituted an Anti-Nepotism Policy
   Anonymous...31
7. What the Army Taught Me About Management
   Fred Taucher..35
8. My Boss Didn't Operate in the Real World
   Illysa Izenberg 39

9. We Changed Our Compensation Plan
   Patti Galloway......................................42
10. Managing Through a Crisis
   Anonymous..46
11. Serving on Nonprofit Boards was Hurting Me
   Deborah Stallings................................49
12. Finding My "A" Employees Fast
   Joe Humphries....................................52
13. I Didn't Know What My Bosses Wanted
   Anonymous..55
14. I Was Afraid of My Employees
   Anonymous..59
15. Retaining My Workers Was Tough
   Anonymous..63
16. My Client Was Sexually Harassed
   by His Female Boss
   Anonymous..66
17. My Employee Was in the Wrong Job
   Steve Jordan......................................72
18. We Had to Find a Compromise
   Robin Cowie.......................................75
19. I Caught the Problem at "Point Easy"
   Susan Weems.......................................79
20. How I Managed a Global Operation
   George D. Wells..................................82
21. I Taught Customer Service to Grunting Teenagers
   Joanie Winberg...................................86

Contents

22. My Direct Reports Were Fighting
    Charlie Bitzis 89

23. I Fired a Drunk
    Anonymous 92

24. I Manage Strong-Willed Entrepreneurs…and Listen
    to Them
    Rick Ritter 96

25. His Sales Masked the People Problem
    Anonymous 99

26. Ask Them the Right Questions
    Kathryn Whitecotton 103

27. Encouraging Competition Got Me Results
    Susan Harlan 107

28. I Fired My Star Employee
    Anonymous 110

29. Mediating Family Issues Made Me Sick
    Norma Owen 113

30. We Bought a Company and Left Former Owners
    in Place
    Anonymous 117

31. I Inherited an Employee Who Hated Me
    Anonymous 120

32. I Put My Family Ahead of My Job
    Ralph Quinn 124

33. The President Tried to Bully Me
    Anonymous 127

34. "We Need to Part Ways" Was Music to My Ears
    Anonymous 131

35. Managing the Start Up of Our Family Brand
Paul, Hermine, Juliette, and Olivia Brindak
....135

36. Getting the Owner of a Family Business to Plan for Succession
Anonymous...138

37. I Made the Tough Ethical Decision
Anonymous...142

38. I Hired the Wrong Person
Clay Nelson 146

39. I Fired a Friend
Marissa Levin 150

40. My Boss Took Care of Me in a Personal Crisis
Nancy Slater 153

41. I Went from Corporate to Cleaner
Kermit Engh 156

42. From "Us" to "Them"
Ellen Rohr 160

43. Establish Diversity Relationships Before You Have a Crisis
Joe Schneider 163

44. Mentors Helped Me Succeed
Carnela Renee Hill.......................................167

45. I Had a Rotten Boss
Anonymous...170

46. Sexual Harassment Was Accepted
   Anonymous..174
47. I Didn't Want to Believe
   Rod Toner...177
48. We Turn Teenagers Around
   Ellen Frederick 180
49. Our Franchisees Didn't Believe I Could Be
   an Effective CEO
   Dina Dwyer-Owens 184
50. Employees Living Their Dream
   Mike Nelson 187

<u>Part Two:</u> What You Can Do About It

Chapter Two: Seventeen Critical Survival Strategies 195
1. Know the Outcome You Want from the
   Resolution of a Conflict with an Employee....195
2. Create a Team of Mentors 196
3. Communicate...197
4. Confront the Bad Issues Immediately.............198
5. You Do Not Have to Be Nice. You Have
   to Be Fair...199
6. Be Clear about Evaluation Criteria 200
7. Have a Sexual Harassment Policy
   and Follow It 201
8. Hire People Who Are Smarter than You Are
  202

9. Encourage Disagreements, Discussions,
   and Debates 202
10. Praise in Public. Punish in Private 202
11. Know How to Manage Different
    Personality Styles 203
12. Take a Calculated Risk 204
13. Keep Family and Business Separate..............204
14. Follow the Employee Policy Manual............205
15. Never Fire Anyone When You Are Mad 211
16. Fire with "Ruthless Compassion" 211
17. Say Thank You 211

**Chapter Three: Six Steps to Successfully Groom Your
                Next Manager..................................213**
Step 1: Decide How Much Information He Needs
       214
Step 2: Introduce the New Manager to His Team
       216
Step 3: Responsibility, Authority,
        and Accountability 217
Step 4: Hard Lessons to Learn 219
Step 5: Hiring...221
Step 6: Firing..223

**Chapter Four: The Seven Greatest Management Myths
        ....225**
Myth 1: Your Employees Can Read Your Mind
       225

Contents

Myth 2: You Can Be Friends With Your Employees 226

Myth 3: Your Employees Have the Same Agenda as You Do 226

Myth 4: Your Employees Have the Same Work Ethic as You Do 227

Myth 5: You Can Change People.......................228

Myth 6: You Can Do It Alone 229

Myth 7: Your Employees Are Irreplaceable........229

Chapter Five: Words of Wisdom.............................231

Acknowledgments...241

Index..243

About the Author 255

THE UGLY TRUTH ABOUT MANAGING PEOPLE

My grandfather taught me that it is much better to learn from the successes and mistakes of others—it shortens your path to success when you do not have to do all the trial and error yourself. *The Ugly Truth about Managing People* is one way to shorten that path. Whether you are an entrepreneur seeking to hire your first employee, or an employee who has just been promoted to manager, or the long-time manager of global operations for a Fortune 500 company, you can take the lessons from this book and apply them to your situation. Learn from what others have done well and what mistakes others have made to save time and avoid frustration on your way to becoming a successful manager. Or, if you have a rotten boss, you might even give him a copy of this book—anonymously, of course.

The Ugly Truth about™ series is about realities, not theories. Sometimes the truth hurts, but it always helps in the long run. These are stories from people who have lived and survived these real situations. They are not fantasies or someone's idea of what could happen; these are real situations that actually did happen and had to be dealt with. We share them so that you, the reader, can follow what we have done well, do not make our mistakes, and take the right actions to prevent circumstances that could hurt emotionally or cause stress and sleepless nights.

While many of the stories are anonymous because of legal and corporate policies, they are all true. Everyone who shared a story has done so with the expressed wish that you, the reader, learn from what he has done well or the mistakes he has made.

It is my hope that you take these lessons, apply them to your management career, and continue to grow and succeed.

Ruth King

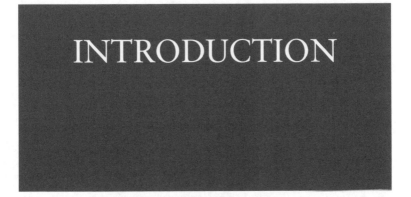

INTRODUCTION

Managing people is one of the toughest jobs in business. With the right managers, there is no limit to how large a business can grow. With the wrong managers, a business can, and probably will, fail.

Every company, from the largest Fortune 500 companies to sole proprietorships, has managers. A Fortune 500 company has multiple layers of managers. Even the chief executive officer (CEO) has to answer to a manager—the board of directors. Sole proprietors, too, have managers. They have to answer to their banker, their customers, and, if they are smart, their advisory board.

The statistics are chilling. The Small Business Administration and other researchers agree that more than 75 percent of all businesses fail within the first five years. Even large companies fail because of mismanagement. Enron and WorldCom are two of the latest examples where managers have caused companies to die. Businesses that need to survive and thrive need good—even, great—managers.

We have all had great managers, who have got the best out of us. They help us in keeping the job interesting, increase productivity, and encourage growth, both personal and professional, all contributing to furthering the growth and profit of the company

Many of us have also had terrible managers. We hated working for that person and even hated coming to work. We have spent as much time focused on finding a way to be promoted or transferred or finding a way to switch companies as we did actually working for that bad boss. The company, too, as a whole, suffers under bad management: many a time, sales and profits do not grow and customers are not happy.

Good managers earn the respect of their workers and are creative, motivated, and fair. They have a sense of purpose, deal well with tough performance issues, and tackle problems head on rather than hoping they will disappear. You will find many other important and useful managerial qualities in the stories shared in this book. Good managers create an environment where employees can do their job productively and positively contribute to the bottom line of the company.

All managers make mistakes; the smart ones learn from theirs and modify their behavior. However, the smartest and the most experienced learn from the mistakes of others before they make the same blunder. *The Ugly Truth about Managing People* reveals some of the actual pitfalls that may lie in wait for a manager. By using good techniques and troubleshooting the bad situations, you will be a better manager and will create a better working environment for people who work with you.

In Part One, you will read stories of managers sharing the good, the bad, and the ugly situations they have dealt with. You will see that good managers and good management teams take excellent care of their customers, no matter what, which helps ensure a company's survival. In Part Two, *What You Can Do About It*, critical management survival strategies are discussed that give you proven methods for resolving challenging situations. Lastly, some words of wisdom from those who are or have been successful managers are presented.

I spoke to many more people than just those whose stories are told here. Many declined to share their experience because of legal ramifications or corporate policy. Those who shared did so with the hope that you use what they did well and avoid doing what they did poorly. All want to help you become a better manager.

The names of many managers and, at certain instances, industries have been changed. The companies that these managers work for range from the very large to the very small. Some of the stories are from employees who had, in their opinion, rotten bosses and explain what you can learn from them (painful, though, it may be). Some are responsible for a team of managers; others are the only managers. Some manage the company, while others manage sales, finance, or operations. Still others manage family businesses. By reading the stories in this book, you will learn what it takes to be a good manager, generate more profits for your company, and make you and everyone around you a success.

CHAPTER ONE

WHY WE ARE MANAGERS

Manager. Management. Boss. These words conjure up lots of mental images, not all of them positive. Many of you have learned how to be a manager from bosses who treated you poorly. The sentence "I learned how to be a good manager because I had a rotten one" has been repeated to me very many times. In fact, poor managers *can* teach you how to be a good manager. I have personally experienced poor managers who have helped me define the type of manager I want to be and hope I am.

I like to watch people succeed. Often I groom young, idealistic college graduates—I give them the freedom to do their job, and sometimes they learn about accountability the hard way. Coaching young managers through their first review and disciplinary action letter they write for a nonperforming employee or their first firing is a management lesson they will use forever.

I knew I had succeeded in becoming a good manager when a iBusinessChannel.com producer, whom I hired out of college, walked into my office one day and said that I had taught her more than she would have gotten in school getting her MBA. She was handing in her resignation to follow her dream. I thanked her and wished her well. I did not argue with her or try to convince her to stay back. I knew enough to let her go. It was time for her to try her next career, and because of me she felt prepared to proceed. That was an enormous compliment.

I want to see everyone working on my team succeed. Everyone has different strengths to be discovered and used accordingly. No one has to be afraid of mistakes—in fact, one of the rules in our policy manual is you are fired if you get caught

Everyone has different strengths to be discovered and used accordingly.

lying. I have enforced this policy in the past. No matter how big the mistake, how costly it will be to fix it, admit it—this applies to all, even me. Everyone knows that admitting failure is far better in the long run. No one in my company is afraid of risking and failing. As long as it is legal, moral, and ethical, we will try almost anything that helps our customers and team members. If it fails, so what? We learn from it, and move on.

Now that you know why I manage, think about why you want to be a manager. Prestige? Power? More money? Many people aspire to be managers; some even want to lead large numbers of people. Do you have what it takes? By reading the stories in this book you will see that the skills needed to manage are usually different from the skills possessed by someone who punches the clock in a 9-to-5 job. In fact, managers often work longer, harder hours than any member of the team they lead.

Are you willing to devote a good portion of your life to taking charge of a team? Can you do the fun parts of your job and the difficult parts? Hiring can be thrilling; firing rarely is.

You might find that you love management. You might find that you hate it and want to go back to what you were doing before you were

Discover why you want to manage: That's the first step in becoming a great manager.

promoted. It is perfectly all right to go back to what you were doing before you became a manager, if you find that you do not like management.

But if you find that you do like management and you want to continue, share your business goals with your boss. He should be supportive of those goals and help you achieve them. He should also help you establish a time frame to achieve those goals and milestones along the way.

For business owners who are managing their own

business, outside advisors can help establish and meet business goals. These goals should be realistic. Advisors should hold you responsible for achieving them and guide you along the way.

Discover why you want to manage: That's the first step in becoming a great manager. Then finish reading *The Ugly Truth About Managing People* to help reduce the mistakes you will make and increase your chances for management success.

PART ONE

50 STORIES OF THE UGLY TRUTH ABOUT MANAGING PEOPLE

1.

I WAS THROWN INTO MANAGEMENT
Lea Strickland
FOCUS Resources

I was one of the few women in an executive training program for a Fortune 500 company and was in the first class that was required to start work in the manufacturing plant. As a woman, I had the option of a rotational assignment working in the plant on the production floor. I accepted it and started as an assistant production supervisor.

I was assigned to second shift, which began at 3:00 a.m. We had fourteen men in our area and were responsible for one-third of the plant revenues. Our team put a product on every vehicle. I took a lot of flack during my first week on the job and was continually teased, but I was actually having fun despite the pranks being pulled on me.

At the beginning of my second week, I arrived to find all fourteen men of our team waiting for me. They told me I was now the supervisor. I said, "Hi guys, nice prank" and started laughing. After all, no one had called me to let me know that the regular supervisor was gone.

They assured me that they were serious. Then I thought, "It is six hours before I will see another supervisor. I can't do inventory. I can't identify the parts. I can't shut down the line and cause millions of dollars in losses. I don't know union rules or who is supposed to do what." But above all, I knew that I had to keep production going.

I told my team: "I'll make you a deal. You've been working in this plant for 20 to 30 years. I've been here a week. You will keep the plant running. I will learn it and figure out how to get you paid."

Six hours later, I voiced my confusion and frustration in the management meeting,. "Why wasn't I notified that I would be supervising?" Their answer, "We knew you would figure it out!"

The fourteen men on my team kept their end of the bargain. They taught me how to do inventory, what machines produced what parts, and told me the things that I was allowed to do and not allowed to do, according to the union. I worked from 2:00 a.m. to 6:00 p.m. every night including weekends. I learned and they learned. We made it. I was constantly just ahead of the assembly lines.

It struck me one day that the men knew which machines produced what products in what amount of time in their heads. I was a spreadsheet MBA person. In my opinion, there had to be a better way to keep track of that crucial information. I got a computer without permission and made everyone agree that it would not disappear.

While they watched, I began recording the function of every machine, the inventory needed, the production times, and made the connections. I used this collection of data to maximize efficiency and production.

The union men found this fascinating. When my calculations were off, they agreed to cover for me (and make more parts) as long as I did not say anything to "management." They saw I was learning fast and willing to help, to clean machines, and do whatever was necessary, so they were willing to help me in return. In addition, I used the computer

It was my responsibility to keep the line running, so it didn't matter who made the mistake; the ultimate fault was mine and I had to fix it.

to determine how to keep the plant rolling and how to do controlled shut downs. I did not have thirty years of experience in my head. I needed the spreadsheet. And it worked.

In management meetings, I stood up for my fourteen men. I accepted the blame for the team rather than holding individuals accountable when mistakes happened. It was my responsibility to keep the line running, so it didn't matter who made the mistake; the ultimate fault was mine and I had to fix it. This was one of the crucial keys to my acceptance. I knew that I had passed muster when I got a nickname—they called me The Lady.

Of course I had rules too. They were not allowed to swear and they had to tell me when mistakes were made. In return, I treated them with respect and acknowledged their abilities. We made a good team. They stood up for me. There were very many people who did not want a woman MBA on the floor. They told me when someone was going to try to do something rebellious so I could prevent it. They told their coworkers not to mess with The Lady because she was okay. I was never grieved by the union.

During my three months on the floor, I once used my spreadsheet to determine when to make a controlled shut down of one production line in order to keep the other lines going. On the way to the management meeting I informed the assembly manager that one of the lines was going down at 10:00 a.m. I had already calculated that we were ahead of the plant that needed the part and that since that plant was going to be idle, we had produced enough parts for their assembly line prior to shut down.

There was shouting and screaming in the meeting—they were sure there was no way I could do this. I assured them that I had modeled it and it was okay. At 9:56 a.m. the line went down with every member of plant management in my area. I was sitting behind the computer and firstly everyone wanted to know where I got it. Then they wanted to see what I had done because the process that I had modeled worked. I was eventually promoted out of the plant.

What I learned:

- I was willing to say "I don't know" and accept that the men had many more years of experience than I did. By asking them to teach me, I got their respect. And I was not afraid to get my hands dirty to learn what I needed to know.

- I treated everyone in the team fairly and with respect.
- By taking responsibility when there was a problem rather than blaming it on a specific person, I gained their trust. They were more willing to help me, since I was helping them.

Applying the lessons learned to your company:

- Have a sense of humor. Had I not been able to laugh at the pranks and teasing, my life could have been miserable.
- Acknowledge what each member of your team contributes. Everyone is important and should understand how he or she fits overall.
- When you are the supervisor you are responsible for the team's performance. If there is a problem, it is your problem and not one individual's problem. When speaking with the management, you must accept responsibility for the team and not blame anyone. Of course, deal with the team member who made the mistake in private.

2.

A WOMAN SEXUALLY HARASSED ME
Anonymous

I was the operations manager for a large wholesaler and had both warehouse and branch responsibilities. The branch was growing rapidly and needed some clerical help, so I authorized the branch manager to hire someone to help in the office. Sue (name changed), after being interviewed, landed the job. She was in her mid twenties and her husband had been in an industrial accident. Sue was desperately trying to make ends meet and needed this full-time job and the benefits.

By all appearances Sue was a hard worker. She generally showed up in jeans and a flannel shirt every day, just like one of the guys. However, she could also put on a dress, bat her eyes, and the men in the warehouse would fall all over her.

I lived about twenty-five miles south of the office and Sue lived about fifteen miles south of me. One day she asked me if she could ride with me because she could not afford the gas. As my wife complained that I work too late everyday, this gave me an excuse to get out of the office earlier. The next day Sue drove to my house in the morning and I drove the rest of the way to work.

This arrangement worked well for about two weeks. Then, one afternoon as we were driving home, Sue started talking. She said, "My husband is incapacitated. I've been so long without a man. We could have a great time together."

I was shocked. I said, "I am your supervisor. I don't want to hear another thing about this. It isn't acceptable behavior and this carpool is done." She responded that the ride home was no longer work and that if I pulled off the road she could show me what she meant.

The next morning I went directly into the owner's office and said, "I need to make you aware of this"

I told her that, in my opinion, this was still work, and that I was going to tell others about what she had said. Sue burst into tears and apologized for bringing it up. By the time we arrived at my house she had convinced me not to say anything.

At dinner I was quiet and distracted. My wife asked me what was going on. When I told her what happened on the ride home she said two things. Firstly, she had never trusted Sue (my wife has an uncanny ability to spot problems). Secondly, she convinced me to write down everything that had happened even though I told Sue I would not say anything to anyone. My wife said that if I did not write down the incident, I would regret it until the day I die. At that time, I did not know how right she was.

That evening I wrote down everything and my wife read it. The next morning I went directly into the owner's office and said, "I need to make you aware of this" and handed him the piece of paper with my description of what had happened the evening before. He immediately called his labor attorney. The owner faxed my document to the attorney. Within a few minutes, the attorney called back and said that the document had to be notarized immediately, and not by our company's notary. The company attorney sent over one of his assistants to notarize the document. He also cautioned us not to say anyone about the incident.

The following weekend, we had a company meeting at a location about one hundred fifty miles away from the branch. Everyone from thirty branches, including Sue, would be attending. When I checked into the hotel I asked who my roommate was going to be and who was in the room next to me. To my shock, Sue and I had adjoining rooms.

I told the desk clerk that I had to be moved. He informed me that this was impossible since there were no vacant rooms in the hotel. I called an old friend who was also attending the meeting and told him that we needed to change rooms. I did not tell him why and asked him to just trust me. We changed rooms.

That evening after the meetings were over, I went to my room. At about 11:00 p.m. I received a telephone call from the friend who had taken my original room. He was laughing. He commented, "I can't believe that you were so nice to me. I got this birthday present. There was a knock on the interlocking door. I opened it and saw Sue standing there buck naked in high heels. I yelled and slammed the door." My friend wanted to know what was going on. I told him nothing, then called the company owner that night and we wrote the incident and notarized statements.

On Tuesday following the weekend meeting, Sue did not show up for work. Instead, we got a letter from an attorney claiming emotional distress, sexual harassment, and embarrassment. The letter further stated that this matter could be settled for $1 million.

The owner called the labor attorney, who told us that this was a scam and that I was being set up. He sent a letter to Sue's attorney attaching the two notarized documents of what had really happened. He assured us that it would be solved and it did.

What I learned:

- My wife was right. My life would have been vastly different had I not listened to her and written down everything.
- Had my attorney not requested that each incident be notarized when it happened, we could have been accused of making it up later. They could have made the case that I was relying on a faulty memory, potentially costing us a million dollars. I was the branch manager and I realized that I should have known better.

Applying the lessons learned to your company:

- Document everything that happens in relation to age, sex, race, creed, and religion, no matter how small or insignificant it might seem. You do not know the motivation of the individual involved and might need the documentation later.
- A notary within your company should not notarize the statements. One that works for an attorney is better.
- Make sure that you have a good labor attorney. The person I hired immediately recognized a potential scam and took steps to protect us.

3.

I CURSED AT MY BOSS
Anonymous

I was the manager for a very busy service department. We were growing by leaps and bounds and I was stressed and overworked. One of the people working for me was not doing her job properly—I was forced to do her job along with mine, and as a result I was lagging behind in getting the mountain of paperwork done. I was looking to replace her. One of the areas of major concern was payroll. I always managed to squeak by with getting it to accounting each week just in time or only a few minutes late.

Some background on my boss, the owner of the company: He is driven to develop top managers. As such, he is very demanding and will push you as far as he can. He wants to see whether you will push back and how you will push back. He has a great relationship with all of the managers who make it through his test.

One day the owner said that he and the office manager wanted to talk with me. When I went to his office he said, "Sit and listen to what I have to say." He immediately started talking and would not let me get a word in edgewise. They were going to write me a warning about not getting payroll in time! I had never been written up in my life and this reason seemed really petty to me. It would have been different if I had been smoking something I should not have been, stealing, or any other equally serious charge. To top it off, I had been asking for help constantly. I kept them updated. My boss and the office manager knew the situation I was in. There should have been no surprises that I was just squeaking by with getting the payroll information in time.

During this tirade from my boss I got more and more enraged. Since he would not let me say anything in my defense, I stood up, stated a few simple facts about the situation, put my hands on his desk and said, "F—- you," turned, and walked out the door.

At this point I fully expected not to have my job anymore. I was so mad that I was crying. I went back to my office and started packing my desk. Then I left the building.

During the drive home I called my boyfriend and said, in tears, "I think we've resolved the working late issue." I told him what happened and that I did not expect to have my job the next morning. I was totally disrespectful and should not have said that, no matter how angry I was.

The next morning I was clearing my desk when my boss came into my office and shut the door. I expected him to fire me. I was shocked when he apologized! He realized that he had pushed me too far and this was my way of pushing back. He said that when I left he did not know whether he wanted to strangle me or hug me. Instead he just looked at me (and the office manager did not say anything either).

This incident was a turning point in our relationship. I then knew that I could say what I needed to say without fear. It opened the door to great communication between the two of us and also I gained respect. I never cursed at him again.

> *He realized that he had pushed me too far and this was my way of pushing back.*

What I learned:

- Take risks only with people whom you have a great relationship with. Had I not built a relationship with my boss, I could never have cursed at him. I probably would have walked out and not said anything.

- The stress of this situation was a turning point and actually allowed us to calmly discuss what happened, the next day. He became a mentor and helped me grow and succeed.

Applying the lessons learned to your company:

- New managers must establish their boundaries. This requires constant and frank communication. You must learn what you can and cannot do to be successful.
- Owners can be wrong. Sometimes it takes an extremely stressful situation for them to realize it. And it takes a strong owner to admit his mistake and address the situation rather than just fire someone.

Some thoughts from my boss:

- It is my nature to push people to see how far I can push them. In this case I realized that I had pushed too far.
- I realized that I needed to give her time to explain what was being done rather than not letting her say anything. Given the stress that she was under, this pushed her over the edge.
- Soon after the incident, I was proud to see that she could stand up for herself. This might not have been the best way to do it, but she definitely got her point across.

4.

WE NEEDED A CLEAR PET POLICY
Richard Woods
Partner, FlexHR

FlexHR provides human resource leadership services for companies that are either too small or do not want a full-time human resources (HR) department. One of our clients is a company that allows pet owners to bring their pets to work. Unfortunately, they did not have a pet policy establishing the proper conduct of pet and owner in the office.

There was a woman in our client's office who was afraid of a male coworker's dog. She was annoyed that the dog kept coming into her office and the owner would not restrain it. She politely complained and asked that he keep his dog in his office and shut his door. He refused to do this. After several complaints, she was given the option to move her office. She replied, "Why should I move my office when all he has to do is to keep his dog in his office with the door shut?"

One day, after repeated complaint the man got belligerent. He threw two boxes of copy paper in front of her door to block his dog from entering her office. He banged on his office wall and screamed and cursed at the woman. Pet or no pet, this was totally unacceptable behavior at work. Unfortunately, no one immediately reprimanded him for his actions. And to provoke an already poor situation, the man sent out an email with his dog's picture and the words, "Please don't persecute me."

Upon investigation I found different people had different agendas. The president of the

Instead of working productively, they were rehashing an unfortunate incident.

company wanted to keep a pet-friendly workplace. Even though having dogs in the office violated the lease, he still wanted everyone to have the liberty to bring their pet to work. Also, the manager did not want to fire the man for inappropriate behavior at work. The man was a great revenue producer and the manager thought he was too valuable to the organization to be dismissed.

The woman also generated much revenue for the company. She wanted a formal, written pet policy for the man to be fired. At this point, the entire office was polarized over the debate.

I mediated this situation and had never seen anything so absurd. Those college-educated people were acting like two-year-olds. Instead of working productively, they were rehashing an unfortunate incident. I thought the man should have been fired for his angry outburst. Clearly, something had to be done.

Firstly, the man got a disciplinary letter that had nothing

to do with his pet. It only dealt with his inappropriate behavior at work. The letter stated that the company will not tolerate screaming, cursing, and banging on walls in the work environment. It included mandatory conflict management training and he was banned from bringing his dog into the office.

A formal pet policy was written and implemented. Even though you would think most of it is common sense, in this case, definitely it needed to be formally written. The major requirement: anyone bringing a pet to work must contain and manage the pet; otherwise, the pet cannot come to work.

What I learned:

- I could not find standard pet policies for the workplace. The San Francisco SPCA has some articles on the positive aspects of pet-friendly policies. However, each company determines its own policies. In addition, I could not find any litigation over pet policies which would have helped shape our policy.
- I thought the man should be fired for grossly unacceptable behavior right after he cursed and threw the boxes of copy paper. This was a total disregard for proper etiquette in the workplace.
- There was too much time between the incident and the disciplinary action—almost three weeks. Action should have been taken immediately. Then the incident

would not have escalated into a major crisis and distracted everyone from work.

Applying the lessons learned to your company:

- If you see inappropriate behavior, take action immediately. If not, a minor incident could become a major crisis and might get blown out of proportion and keep your workers from doing their jobs.
- If your company allows pets in the office, make sure that you are compliant with your lease and that you create a formal policy outlining pet behavior and consequences for inappropriate behavior.

5.

I MANAGED CHILDISH PEOPLE
Mark Miller

I had just turned thirty and was a sales person handling the southern territory for an instrument company. I was very good at selling and pulled in high commissions. As a result, I was recognized for my sales ability. One day I got a call summoning me to the main office. I flew to Pittsburgh from Houston and was offered the Pittsburgh district sales manager position. My boss sold me on the promotion. I bought.

Driving back to the airport I realized that I did not know anything about management. The company did not have a training program, so I was on my own. I literally picked up a management book at the airport and read it on the airplane. Little did I realize that I was taking on more headaches, less commission, and four "kids" who were an average of ten years older than me.

The older salesmen severely tested me. They mocked me with lines like "Since you're such a great salesman, what would you do in this situation?" They pretended that they did not know how to sell. I spent hours traveling and on the telephone with them. They tried to swindle things from the company that they had not earned, such as trips to trade shows in Las Vegas. And I was sure they were laughing behind my back. I was the new kid sales manager who did not know much.

The sales people were getting away with things they should not be. They would not sell without my help. They "forgot" to turn in sales reports. One day it dawned on me that managing those salespeople was like raising children: If you let them get away with everything, you will have spoiled brats. I had spoiled brats that I had to reign over.

I learned to discipline them. I decided not to pay attention to them when they did not turn in their call reports and other paperwork. I did, however, make one major mistake—I did not help them close deals. By not helping them close deals, everyone lost: they may not have made commission, but the company also lost profit. I quickly reversed this discipline tactic.

My boss was of no help; I was out there on my own. I eventually found people in other companies in similar positions that I could talk with. It was great to have people to bounce ideas off of who had undergone similar experience.

I also got help from an unexpected place. My wife was an ele-

> *Her rules of clearly communicating expectations, immediately praising good behavior, and immediately punishing bad behavior worked.*

mentary school teacher. She talked to me about how she achieved control and discipline in the classroom. I found that I could apply some of her techniques in the workplace. After all, my salespeople were acting like children. Her rules of clearly communicating expectations, immediately praising good behavior, and immediately punishing bad behavior worked.

After my first six months of making mistakes and learning, I slowly began earning the respect of the salespeople. Within a year their sales went up and the Pittsburgh district sales improved overall. Because I had done a good job I was promoted to a higher position in New Jersey.

What I learned:

- Managing resentful, immature people takes the same skill set as raising kids: You have to be nurturing, mentoring, and coaching to succeed.
- I realized that a large part of my job was to keep them happy. I needed to help them through the inevitable highs and lows of the sales cycle so that they could earn money, instead of getting them to focus on turning in sales reports on time.

Applying the lessons learned to your company:

- Acquire the necessary management skills as quickly as you can. If need be, beg and plead for management training. If your company does not have a training program, find an outside one (such as Sandler Selling Systems' Strategic Sales Management program).
- Salespeople need coaching more than supervising. Good sales people develop the necessary skills to cheer themselves on most of the time, but you have got to help them see the bigger picture and attain their goals rather than micromanage them on a day-to-day basis.

6.

I INSTITUTED AN ANTI-NEPOTISM POLICY
Anonymous

I joined a division of a growing defense contractor as the head of human resources. The day I started, my division had 1,500 employees; it had grown to 2,500 employees by the time I left. One major issue I had to solve was that the company did not have all of the people it needed because of our high turnover rate—once they were adequately trained, people tended to leave us in the lurch.

Upon investigation, I found a series of issues contributing to this problem. The most critical, from my perspective, was that nepotism was rampant throughout management. Managers hired husbands, wives, sons, daughters, cousins, and other family members. These family members were in the same department and often worked for each other. People were not advancing because of merit, but because they knew someone. From what I could determine, the best jobs were going to relatives rather than people who earned them through stellar job performance. Those talented people were leaving because they were not advancing though they were working hard.

There were fights in the lobby between husbands and wives. A secretary's ex-husband was stalking her. This could not continue if the division had to grow and meet business goals. The final blow was when a production manager hired her extramarital lover. She ended up divorcing her husband and marrying her lover privately. The marriage was eventually discovered, as was the fact that she had hired and promoted him. There was outrage.

My solution to these issues was writing an anti-nepotism policy. I knew I had to sell it to the division leadership team first. Permission to implement this policy took a lot of persuasion and selling to my bosses; their concern was that we could not find enough qualified people to hire into our rapidly growing operation, and that this might hinder the process even more. What eventually convinced them was my assertion that better control over hiring processes could save on training costs, improve morale, and increase performance.

> *What eventually convinced them was my assertion that better control over hiring processes could save on training costs, improve morale, and increase performance.*

I used the examples of the domestic fights in the lobby and documented the turnover (discovered through exit interviews), explaining how qualified people were not getting chances for advancement because they were not related to their manager. But this had to stop. I promised that the turnover rate would go down when this policy was implemented and my bosses finally agreed.

I thought that I had a hard sell to my bosses, but convincing my team leaders and department managers that this was the best policy was nearly impossible. Of course, they wanted to continue their practice of hiring family members. They hated me and complained to my bosses, but to no avail.

I moved the company toward three objectives: (1) hiring based on potential, credentials, and history of success; (2) promotion

Leadership needed to recognize and reward the right behaviors.

as a reward for performance and contribution; and (3) merit salary increases based on accomplishment against fairly assigned objectives rather than bloodlines. Leadership needed to recognize and reward the right behaviors. My anti-nepotism policy turned out to be the catalyst for the change we needed.

The first step was grandfathering in all of the existing family members so that they could stay in the company; however, family members were no longer able to work directly for each other and preferably were not even in the same department.

The new policy generated fair performance reviews and fair merit increases, and the upper management started to realize what I promised would happen— decreased turnover.

What I learned:

- Hiring family members is never a solution to the problem of not being able to meet your hiring goals, especially in a large, publicly traded company; in fact, it often actively works against you. Hiring goals must always be tied to sound talent retention strategies. Having a fair and unbiased leadership team is critical.

- You have to do what is right. I saw talented people leaving the company because they were not being treated fairly and because of people getting raises not due to merit but because they were family members. I fought for changes, and even though it took six years of hard work for the effort to evolve completely, it was worth it. The policy is still in place today and is now coupled with many other fair and consistent practices that build loyalty, higher performance, and ever-improving morale.

- Even in human resources, patience and selling are necessary skills. You have to be able to sell your ideas and beliefs both to the upper management and the other managers and to those you employ. There could be resistance to new policies, and you have to know how to deal with it.

Applying the lessons learned to your company:

- Family members should not be working together. Most large companies have a policy stating that if two employees get married and are in the same department, one of the two has to leave that department.
- In smaller companies and family-owned businesses, separating family members may not be feasible. You have to be extremely careful not to show favoritism toward family members—you do not want good talent to leave because they think they can never get ahead in such environment.
- Anti-nepotism policies do not apply in all situations. Some family-owned businesses handle this issue well and have loyal, hardworking nonfamily employees.

7.

WHAT THE ARMY TAUGHT ME ABOUT MANAGEMENT
Fred Taucher

I am a Holocaust survivor. I arrived in the United States in September 1946, thirteen years old, with plans to live with my cousins in Missouri. I thought all Americans were rich, but when I arrived in New York and found beggars on the streets, I vowed that if I ever got in a position to help people I would do it. This was the beginning of my management plan. However, the Army had an even greater influence on me.

I graduated from high school and joined the Army. I was sent to Korea, where my job was to track casualties on IBM punch card equipment. These tabulators were programmed with plug boards and wiring. Computers, as we know of them today, were nonexistent. One day, the officer working with me disappeared and I was given a battlefield promotion to warrant officer. An enlisted man was assigned to help me.

The management lessons began. Firstly, never give an order if you are not willing to do the job yourself. I am willing to do all of the jobs in my company. In fact, similar to a computer company, we have had to reinvent ourselves every five years or so to take advantage of the latest in technology. Back in the 1960s we were working on mainframes and had twenty-four-hour shifts. I routinely came to the office at 1:00 a.m. or 2:00 a.m. so that each shift could see me, talk with me, and know that I was there to help.

I am willing to do all of the jobs in my company.

Secondly, do not form a first opinion—find out all the details before you make up your mind. In 1976 I hired a young man who had just been discharged from the Navy. His brother's company was one of our clients and he had given the young man a strong recommendation. When he came for the interview he said, "My brother said to see you but you don't need anybody do you?" I was shocked at the blunt question but hired him despite his inability to interview properly. Why? I knew his brother's work ethic so I did not form an opinion until I saw this young man on the job. He was my first male key punch operator. I put him on the night shift working for a woman supervisor who was amazed that he was so good and got along with everyone. Today, he is the supervisor for our company.

Don't make someone feel inferior.

Thirdly, respect everyone. Don't make someone feel inferior. The Army constantly reminded us to think back to when we were in the position of the enlisted men under us. What was it like for us? Remember how you felt and treat others accordingly.

I constantly use these lessons in the management of our company. I show dedication to the employees. I am always accessible and pay them a decent wage with good benefits. They do not have to worry about keeping a roof over their heads. We work together as a team; they work with me, not for me. This distinction is critical in creating an environment where everyone is happily productive most of the time.

What I learned:

- I know that our company is only as good as our employees. Keeping a positive work environment is critical to success. I try to treat everyone as family as much as possible. I know what is going on in their lives outside of work and how it might affect their performance.
- I detest prejudice. I give people the benefit of the doubt until they prove otherwise. Know what a person is really like before forming an opinion.
- Show dedication. My employees know I am there for them. When they have problems that need to be resolved, they know they can count on me.

Applying the lessons learned to your company:

- Create a team environment. You, as the leader, set the tone. If you enjoy what you are doing, everyone in the team sees it and will have a positive attitude. To be successful you need everyone pulling in the same direction. Have everyone work with you rather than for you.
- Treating your employees with respect spills over to your customers. If your customers see a great team environment, they are more comfortable with you and are more likely to give you repeat business.

8.

MY BOSS DIDN'T OPERATE IN THE REAL WORLD
Illysa Izenberg
Strategy and Training Partners, LLC

Early in my career I was the controller for the entertainment division of a publicly traded company. I found out the hard way that my boss, the president of the division, could not stand to be disagreed with in a meeting. We were in a meeting with about fifteen people and he wanted to do something that was illegal. I told him that he could not do that and he replied, "Well, Illysa, you must have failed finance to have that response." This was totally untrue and embarrassing.

After the meeting I watched people go into his office. Within a few weeks I realized that the real decisions were made during the private *I made sure that I was the last person in so that the decision about what was done would be mine.*

meetings after the public meeting. The last person who went in got the decision swayed in his favor.

Since I had the office across his, I watched who went in and out after the meetings. I made sure that I was the last person in so that the decision about what was done would be mine. In addition, I never confronted or challenged him directly. It was always, "You might want to think about it this way…"

I was also responsible for the profit and loss statement for the division. I had to make sure that we stayed on budget from both a revenue and an expense standpoint. One day I received a huge depreciation charge from the corporate office. It looked as if our division had spent $1 million. I called my contact in accounting and told him it must be a mistake. But he disagreed.

I spent the entire weekend going through the purchase orders looking for purchases without my signature. I could not find them. The following Monday I went into my boss's office and told him about the million dollar purchase. He told me, "Start with Steve [name changed] and find out." I asked why. He said that Steve was a divorced man and you cannot trust a divorced man. I was shocked at this comment. Steve was a competent person. I could only imagine what his thoughts were about others in our division.

I eventually found the million dollars. It was my boss! It turned out that he had spent it on his pet projects without my knowledge. And those projects were not in the budget. When I confronted him about the purchases, his comment was, "I don't need approval from my controller to spend money."

I explained to him that if he did not tell me, then I could not create accurate financial statements and we could not stay on budget. It was clear by this point that the man lived in his own world and was determined not to let a little thing like reality bother him. I wanted out, but he refused to let me move when another division president requested me to join him. Revenues were up and expenses were down under my financial management. However, I did find a way to work for another division and made a lateral move to get out from under his thumb. His division went bankrupt a year later and he lost his job.

What I learned:

- This negative experience taught me how not to be a manager. I use this lesson in the classes I teach on managing conflict.
- Presidents of divisions may have the authority to spend as much money as they want, but if they are smart, they will spend within the confines of the budget. And they should always get input before they spend money on pet projects.

Applying the lessons learned to your company:

- Healthy discussions and disagreements are critical for the success of a company. If your team just rubber stamps your decisions without discussion and debate, you are not as likely to make good decisions—collaboration and discussion help evolve ideas to their very best.

- If you have hired a controller, let that person control. If you spend money you need to let that person know so that there are no surprises later.

9.

WE CHANGED OUR COMPENSATION PLAN
Patti Galloway
Designs Down Under

My husband and I are corporate refugees. We started our remodeling company by accident and tried to apply the corporate management rules that we knew to construction. It was a big mistake.

We were sick of dealing with remodelers and knew we could do a better job. We also knew we did not know construction, so we worked with a builder who was willing to do construction while we did the design.

The business took off and soon we had ten employees. Being from the corporate world we hired workers and treated them as if they were in corporate America. We were used to people working on salary and doing their jobs without much supervision. We did not know yet that construction workers required constant supervision.

We hired on a handshake. We paid for their lunch time and lunches. We paid people based on what their time sheets said rather than checking on their work. If someone promised to get a job done by Thursday, we believed that person rather than asking questions and checking in.

When we started looking at the cost per job, we knew we had a problem. The jobs were coming in over-budget on labor hours. The men in the field were not producing the work in the time allotted. We were not

It was obvious that we were trying to treat our laborers as corporate employees rather than hourly workers.

making profit. We realized if things did not change, we would be out of business soon.

I joined the Raleigh Remodeler's Council and started talking with others in the industry to find out what they were doing differently. Another remodeler within the council spent time with me and pointed out the mistakes we made. It was obvious that we were trying to treat our laborers as corporate employees rather than hourly workers. This had to change.

As a result, we totally revamped our subcontractor payment method. We went from paying hourly wages to paying by the job and providing worker's compensation and liability insurance to requiring the people working on our jobs to provide those insurances. It was a 180-degree turn around and totally necessary for the company to survive.

We were not happy with our supervisor's ability to manage, close the jobs, and oversee the workers; he just did not have the skills to be a superintendent. We requested him to leave, and when he did, we agreed he could pay us back for the truck we purchased for him on a payment plan, again with a handshake. He never made any payments and we did not have anything in writing; he stole our truck. We took him to court and won. Every other employee except one left as well; they knew that the gravy train was over and that they could not take advantage of us any more.

Our customers never knew the difference. There was not even a ripple when we made the change over. We had a backup plan just in case the employees left when we made the change, but thankfully we did not have to use it. Thanks to our builder and to the remodeling council, we had found good people who would work with us on a per job or bid basis. We still use these subcontractors today.

Changing the subcontractor and the estimating and budgeting method turned out to be a great move for us. Our jobs were again profitable and we did not have the stress of always making sure our employees were doing their work efficiently.

What I learned:

- Find a mentor who can help you. Because someone took me under her wing and showed me what I was doing wrong, I was able to change how we approached our labor force. Without her, we probably would not still be in business today. Meeting people and joining associations can help, particularly for smaller companies.

- Numbers tell the productivity story. Without tracking our hours, we never would have known whether our employees were doing their jobs in the allotted time. Once we knew what the reality was we could make the right decisions.

Applying the lessons learned to your company:

- If you are drastically changing your compensation plan, make sure you have a backup if the employees leave. You still need to take care of your customers during the transition.
- In construction, it is difficult to find reliable people to work on your projects. Building a good reputation helps so that people want to work for you. Also, ask for referrals from other companies that you know do good work.

10.

MANAGING THROUGH A CRISIS
Anonymous

On December 15, 2006, at 4:45 a.m., my world as I knew it stopped. My husband woke me up and asked me to take him to the hospital—he had chest pain that wouldn't go away. To make a long story short, the Wednesday before Christmas he had quadruple bypass surgery.

At that point, I knew that I couldn't focus, concentrate, or even really care about my business until the crisis was over. Family is more important; it always has been, and I've stressed that to all fifteen of our employees. However, I never thought I would be the person who needed to take time off for a family emergency.

The timing couldn't have been worse—we were in the middle of a major upgrade to our company's hardware and software systems. I just couldn't deal with it right then. I wondered how the critical project would progress and how my employees would function without me, but I had to be with my husband.

Two people stepped in to run the company while I was gone. One was the project manager for the upgrade (who was working on a contractual basis), and the other was one of my advisors. I sent an email to all of the employees at 3:00 a.m. on a Saturday morning, letting them know that I was stepping down for a while and that the two were now in charge. The following Monday they had a meeting with all of the employees and stressed that the project would continue and that everyone was to continue doing the tasks they had been working on before I left.

For a few days everything went smoothly, but then problems began to crop up. I had made a mistake by putting two people in charge; when one of the employees didn't like what one of the managers said, they'd go to the other. On top of that, one of the employ-

> *I had made a mistake by putting two people in charge; when one of the employees didn't like what one of the managers said, they'd go to the other.*

ees couldn't handle the fact that I didn't put him in charge and started causing disruptions.

I realized my mistake and rectified it—I promoted the person who was project manager to Vice President of Operations. My advisor only wanted to work part-time and didn't want to take day-to-day control, so that person readily agreed to step down as a manager. They had a meeting with the employee who was causing disruptions and clearly explained what was expected of him. Unfortunately, the employee still didn't do his job and was fired.

The Vice President of Operations continues to run the day-to-day business details. He has freed me up to take care of my husband and to do the things that are really important to the growth of the business, such as networking, research, and development, without worrying about the specifics.

What I learned:

- You must have people you can trust who can step in and run your business if you are unable to. I was lucky that I had a good relationship with the project manager and a great advisory board. Employees need to see a smoothly operating business even during a personal crisis.
- Two people cannot be in control. There can only be one decision-maker.
- That strong wake-up call forced my husband and me to look at what was really important to both of us. Business is still very much a part of our lives—we like doing our jobs and seeing others succeed as a result of our efforts. However, I now have a person in place to deal with most of the day-to-day operations so I can concentrate on doing what I need to do with the business, as well as be able to spend plenty of time away from it.

Applying the lessons learned to your business:

- Develop managerial potential in the people under you. If none of your managers has the capability to take over for you on a day-to-day basis in your absence, you need to designate someone outside your business or team who is familiar with what you do and is willing to step in.
- Decide what is important to you. If you want to build a management team and a business, do it. If

you are unhappy, find something that will make you happy. And if something in your personal life makes you realize that you aren't concentrating on the most important things in life, be ready to take a step back from your business.

11.

SERVING ON NONPROFIT BOARDS WAS HURTING ME
Deborah Stallings
HR Anew
www.hranew.com

About two years after I started my business I started getting invitations to serve on corporate boards. I was flattered and said yes to each one. Before I knew it I was on four nonprofit boards.

I was totally naïve. I had no clue what the real expectations were. I discovered that there were both stated and hidden financial commitments and a lot

> *I discovered that there were both stated and hidden financial commitments and a lot more work than I expected.*

more work than I expected. Since I owned a small business, undercapitalized, and understaffed, the board work and financial commitments were solely my responsibility.

I met with my staff to explain that my serving on boards was one way that we were going to market ourselves. Since we did not have the money to commit to a major marketing campaign, serving on boards was a method by which the company could get known. I explained that there would be times that I was unavailable because of these commitments. They understood and readily pitched in if I asked. I did not ask often because they were so busy themselves. And they did not resent the time that I spent away from the business because I communicated what I was doing and why I was doing it.

After I started serving on nonprofit boards, the business revenues took a downturn. I thought it was the economy or just a business cycle we were in. My accountant was instrumental in helping me realize what was actually going on. HR Anew is an 8A certified government contractor. As such, we must track our time and allowable expenses to get paid. My accountant explained to me the number of hours I was spending on outside board activities and told me that my allocation of time had to change if the company had to survive.

I rescheduled my activities immediately. I became choosy about what I committed to and restructured my existing commitments. I delegated more and supervised the activities rather than did the work. Instead of chairing specific functions I mostly chose projects that lasted four to six weeks with only an occasional project that lasted longer.

The most important thing was that I redirected my attention and primary time allocation to HR Anew. I explained to my staff the changes I made and why those changes were made. Again they supported my decision (and probably with a sigh of relief). They had seen how much time these commitments have taken and were glad that I was going to spend more time with them. The company began growing again.

I still sit on nonprofit boards because I believe in giving back. However, I am very much aware of the time and financial commitments and how these may affect my business operations. I guard my time jealously.

What I learned:

- Being asked to serve on boards was very flattering and a boost to my self-esteem, but I had to learn to better manage my time and balance my commitments with business and family.
- My most valuable resources are my time and my health. When I realized how much weight I was gaining as a result of all the food commitments, I hired a personal trainer and am now much more conscious about what I eat at these functions.
- Outside advisors can help you see the forest through the trees. My accountant was strong enough to sit

me down, show me what I was doing, and help me see that I was hurting my company.

Applying the lessons learned to your company:

- Communication is critical. If you are going to spend time away from your business, you need to tell the staff what you are doing and why you are doing it. Then you must get their opinion on it. If you start to see resentment, you have to address it immediately.
- Find good advisors for your business. They should see things from an outside perspective and be willing to counsel you on your errors. You need to count on them for their oversight and opinions.

12.

FINDING MY "A" EMPLOYEES FAST
Joe Humphries

I am addicted to turning around unsuccessful businesses. Once you get through one and are successful, they get in your blood. They also teach you how to work well with people. I was running a large distribution center (DC) in Memphis, Tennessee. The operation was not meeting deadlines, and it was not profitable. I was given the assignment to turn it around.

I knew the expectations for the company—but the employees working to service our customers didn't. I had to shut down the operation for a few hours to hold a department-wide meeting. This was an expensive decision because the company would lose even more profits during the shut down. However, this time was critical. I

I knew the expectations for the company—but the employees working to service our customers didn't.

could not explain what the expectations were if people could not pay total attention to what I was saying, and without these explanations I could not expect the workers to know what was required to transform this center.

At the meeting, and with the employees' input, we decided to establish safety and customer service goals, productivity goals, and profitability goals. I posted these goals every week and ranked everyone using a standard grading scale so that people could see where they stood. Initially I estimated that I had 20 percent As, 30 percent Bs, and 50 percent Cs.

The key was to concentrate on the A people. They were already taking the responsibility and accountability for their work. I showered more attention on them. Soon the Bs and Cs complained that they were not getting the attention the As were getting and that they wanted the same treatment. I explained that they had to become As to get the same treatment and explained what it took to become an A.

I could not make the changes alone. In an organization with several hundred employees, I needed help developing the current As and helping other people become As. I ended up discovering some quality, high performance managers. Some were right in front of me. Many of the initial As who were there when I took over this operation became my "lieutenants."

I made it clear to my lieutenants that it was their job to help mold their team members into the As who were needed for the company to survive. With their help, many of the employees took our training and advice, did what they needed to do, and became As. Within ninety days, I began to see vast improvements and within a year we had only 5 percent Cs.

What did I do with the Cs? I fired them. They did not belong as part of the team, since they were costing the company money.

What I learned:

- Poor performers do not leave. You have to run them off. Good performers will leave on their own if the expectations are not clearly defined.
- People want to follow great leaders. They want direction and discipline. The reality is that they are not happy when they can get away with things they know they should not be able to get away with.
- People want ownership. They want to be involved

and understand where the company is going and how it plans to get where it wants to go.

Applying the lessons learned to your company:

- You must deal with performance issues in a timely manner. If you see good performance, reward it. If you see poor performance, address it immediately with the desired corrections.
- Communicate your expectations well. People need to understand how their work will be judged.
- Do not try to find people who are mirror images of yourself. Find people who can perform and empower them to develop their team under the guidelines you set.

13.

I DIDN'T KNOW WHAT MY BOSSES WANTED
Anonymous

In 1989 I was hired as a programmer for a Fortune 500 Company in the transportation industry. After completing a grueling eight-week training course, I was assigned to work on a proprietary software development language. The programs I wrote were used by our customers and employees.

When I was hired, my managers knew that I had significant experience creating presentations. Some history: In 1989 DOS was still the prevalent operating system. Windows was not in use in my company and the presentation tools available took significant amount of time to create and use. Drag and drop had not been invented yet. As a result of this unique skill I was asked by my supervisor Joan (name changed) to help our development team create presentations to senior management on the status of our projects. I became the creator of the messages sent out by our organization. I did not deliver the presentations; I just created them for Joan and my manager Steve (name changed).

They delivered the presentations in a multimillion dollar media room that got little use until I started creating the presentations. Steve and Joan did not have to do much to give the presentations except hit the spacebar when they were ready to move to the next slide. I incorporated special effects and made them very eye catching and informative. Both Steve and Joan received numerous accolades for their "work" on the presentations. Senior management cited them as examples of how the rest of IT should communicate with them. I was elated. I had helped both my supervisor and my manager get noticed in several positive ways. At Steve's and Joan's request, I continued to provide these presentations on a regular basis and therefore spent most of my time developing them rather than developing software.

I received zero complaints about how I spent my time

and was given periodic "attaboys" for my work. When I completed my first year, I was excited because I expected to get a positive review. I was shocked when Steve gave me a less-than-satisfactory review. One reason was cited: I had not generated enough proprietary code. I was told that I had been hired to write the proprietary code and not to develop presentations.

Not only had Steve received numerous accolades for my work, he had assigned me to it!

In my opinion, this review was totally unfair. Not only had Steve received numerous accolades for my work, he had assigned me to it! In addition, he had deliberately not assigned me work on the proprietary code so that I would have the time to work on the presentations. He even made sure I had a high-powered computer and my own printer (not common in those days) so that I could do more for him.

When I reminded him of that fact, he simply stated that I was measured on the code I developed and therefore his hands were tied. I then asked him if he expected me to continue to provide those presentations/reports. Steve was genuinely flabbergasted. I explained to him that since my performance was measured on my work writing the proprietary code, I would naturally be focusing my attention on writing that code. I offered to teach someone else to do the presentation work and that I would no longer be available to do it.

As I left my performance review, I was so angry that I decided to leave the company. However, before the day was over, I was offered another better job within the company because of my performance on Steve's team. I stayed in my new job.

What I learned:

- Get your duties and what you will be evaluated on in writing. If I had known in the beginning that my performance would be evaluated on the proprietary software I was writing, I would not have accepted the assignment to create the presentations without a change in my job description.
- Even though Steve and Joan got the accolades, word leaked out about who was actually creating the presentations and meeting the deadlines. This was fortunate because as a result of my work, even though it was not what I was supposed to be doing, I got the opportunity for a promotion.
- I was surprised and emotional as I left Steve's office. The knee jerk "I'll leave the company" was not a rational decision since I enjoyed working for the company. I just did not want to work for Steve anymore.
- I had expected that by helping my supervisor and manager to get positive results in their careers, I would be getting a positive review. I was wrong.

Applying the lessons learned to your company:

- Job duties and the tasks that an employee will be evaluated on should be in writing. Both parties should agree on expectations and deliverables, and when these change, amendments should be made to the job description so that there are no surprises during reviews.
- If you are asked to deviate from the agreed-upon expectations, ask how the change will affect your performance measurement. Then, decide whether you want the new assignment in addition to your existing work duties and clarify if you will be evaluated on both.

14.

I WAS AFRAID OF MY EMPLOYEES
Anonymous

I started a spa after working for one for several years. I had lots of repeat customers who knew me and encouraged me to open my own spa. I ran it profitably for a few years before I sold it. Even though it was profitable from a financial standpoint, it was a disaster from the management standpoint.

I had never been a manager before. All of a sudden I

was boss to employees I had worked with as an employee. I was used to being on their level and still wanted the same relationship. In hindsight I realize that, as the boss, my employees could never be on my level and that I couldn't have the same type of relationship with them that I had when we worked together. However, back then, I let my employees walk all over me.

Here is what happened: My spa business was in a small town, and I was afraid it would be hard to find employees who took care of our customers the way that I wanted them to. In essence, I was afraid that my employees would leave and thought that I would not be able to replace them and all the work of the spa would fall on me.

I panicked every time someone threatened to quit and did whatever it required to retain her. This was the wrong message to send. After a few times the employees knew they could get anything they wanted just by threatening to quit.

> *In hindsight I realize that, as the boss, my employees could never be on my level and that I couldn't have the same type of relationship with them that I had when we worked together.*

In addition, I wanted my employees to be happy. I felt that if they were not happy they would leave. I never said, "These are the rules. This is how our business works." I let the employees set their own rules. It was a disaster.

I never disciplined the employee if she was late for a customer's appointment. Therefore, it became acceptable to be late. If someone was late for a customer appointment, I took care of that customer. If someone did not want to come in early for a meeting, I accepted it without disciplining. Soon employees were

The business was still profitable from a financial standpoint but after a year of running it I was miserable.

coming and going as they pleased, with total disregard for their time commitments. It was chaos.

I did not want to fight with my employees. Rather than holding them accountable for their jobs, I did the extra work. I sat back, let it happen, and did not say a word. I got frustrated but never expressed the frustrations.

Customers never noted my dilemma—as far as they knew, everything was fine. The business was still profitable from a financial standpoint but after a year of running it I was miserable. My employees and my customers were happy, but I was tired, overworked, and did not want to deal with my employees anymore.

My accountant came up with a solution: He bought the business. The irony was that he wanted me to stay on as manager. In retrospect, he knew that I could take care of the customers. I just could not take care of the employees. He stated: "If someone has a problem turn it over to me. I'll handle the situation." This was music to my ears. I no longer had to manage people. I could just manage the customers.

What I learned:

- I had to establish rules for the business. Without rules there was anarchy. People came and went as they pleased.
- When someone threatened to quit, I should have said, "There's the door." It would have been the last time someone tried that tactic. I also needed to realize I could have found a qualified replacement.
- Even though the business was financially profitable, my emotional health was critical to its survival.
- Managing employees is different compared to being on their level. Wanting everyone to be happy was a pipe dream; sometimes, you just have to put your foot down.

Applying the lessons learned to your company:

- You cannot be friends with your employees. You have to recognize the power you have over them and they need to respect that power. If you are the boss, you set the rules.
- If an employee threatens to quit, even if he is your most productive employee, let that person quit. If you do not, you will establish that anyone can threaten to quit to get what he wants.

15.

RETAINING MY WORKERS WAS TOUGH
Anonymous

I manage a series of small hotels in the Kansas City area. Our major problem was finding and retaining hotel workers. Even though we pay higher than the prevailing rate for housekeepers and other hotel staff, we had to find a way to motivate them to stay. Here are some of the things that we had done.

Firstly, we had a problem attracting labor. We found that one of our major stumbling blocks was access to affordable, safe day care for our employees' children. In 1988, our company took this issue to the Chamber of Commerce in Overland, Kansas (a suburb of Kansas City). They researched the issue and worked with the Chamber of Commerce in Kansas City, Missouri.

The solution? The chamber found a vacant building which could be turned into a day care and the state, city, and local governments worked together to create the facility. Our employees dropped their children off at the day care center and took a bus to the hotel they were working in and returned to the day care in the evening. This solved one issue: We soon found employees who were willing to work because they had access to safe, childcare without worrying about their children or imposing a burden on their families.

Once we found workers, retention and productivity were the next issues. Turnover could kill us, as could unproductive workers. We worked to solve these two problems. We discovered that money was an issue. Even though our company paid higher than minimum wage, our employees often came to work without breakfast and did not eat all day—they did not have anything at home or they could not afford an $8 lunch. If they did eat, we noticed that they went to local convenience stores and ate "junk." We decided to do a test. We provided breakfast. This did not cost very much, and within a very short time we found that our employees' productivity increased from 10 percent to 15 percent. When some of the hotel managers questioned this expense we showed them that the increase in productivity was greater than the cost of the food. They agreed and supported the program.

Once we found workers, retention and productivity were the next issues.

We then knew that food was a good motivator. How could we use food incentives to increase performance? Pizza parties. After the rooms were cleaned we inspected for quality assurance. We established a "Good Inspections" contest, the reward of which was a pizza party. The room quality rate went up again.

We also care about our employees. Once a woman got a gash in her leg at home. Most of our employees, including this woman, could not afford the deductible for health insurance, so they do not have any. She decided to take a needle and thread and sew up the gash herself. I had the opportunity to visit this hotel and saw her limping. I asked her what was wrong and she showed me her leg. It was infected and she did not have the money to get it fixed. We paid the doctor bills to get the doctor bills to get

> *We always try to do what we can for the employees while watching the profitability of each hotel.*

her leg fixed. She has a scar, but has become an incredibly loyal employee and has told this story of how we take care of our employees over and over again. We always try to do what we can for the employees while watching the profitability of each hotel.

What I learned:

- By providing breakfast and other food items we were able to take care of our employees in a cost-effective way that did not hurt our profitability. It actually helps it.
- Sometimes noncash incentives are more powerful than cash. Would they like a raise? Of course. However, we have to be mindful of the median wages in the area as well as what we can afford to pay and still be profitable. The food is greatly appreciated and increases productivity on the job.

Applying the lessons learned to your company:

- Day care centers for children are a continuing problem for middle and lower class workers. This innovative solution was the result of many local governments working together to solve a problem. It can be replicated anywhere in the United States where there is a vacant building and grandparents who are willing to help.
- If raising a person's salary cannot be done, find non-cash incentives to retain employees. Sometimes, as in this story, food can be the answer. Other answers might include a day off or a gift card for food or other merchandise.

16.

MY CLIENT WAS SEXUALLY HARASSED BY HIS FEMALE BOSS
Anonymous

Jake (name changed) came into my office after he was fired by his boss, Elizabeth (name changed). He had spent ten years with the company and had been promoted to a management position. His record was good, as evidenced by positive performance appraisals. Jake's story was one of disparate treatment based on sex—specifically, Jake's refusal to have sex with his female boss.

Jake's termination letter said that he was being fired because of a pattern of being repeatedly late for work, but this did not seem right. Yes, he had been late a few times. However, there were many of his female teammates who were not disciplined for tardiness. In fact, the women repeatedly signed each other in and took great liberties with the com-

As far as Jake could see, not a single female was reprimanded for tardiness, and each essentially could come and go as she pleased.

pany's flextime policy. As far as Jake could see, not a single female was reprimanded for tardiness, and each essentially could come and go as she pleased. He was the only one singled out, written up, and fired for being late the slightest bit. This made Jake think that he was being fired for spurning Elizabeth's sexual advances.

Jake had known Elizabeth the entire time he had worked at the company. She had been married to another employee for most of her tenure, and during that time, the relationship between Jake and Elizabeth had been purely professional. After her divorce, however, Elizabeth frequently bemoaned how she had been "taken to the cleaners" and seemed to manifest a more callous attitude toward men. Due to her demanding job, she traveled often and did not have much time to look outside the company for a love interest; therefore, she soon turned her attention to those within—specifically Jake.

The first time Elizabeth approached Jake was during a coworker's housewarming party. He went upstairs to use the rest room and Elizabeth jumped into his arms at the top of the stairs. Jake, surprised, dropped her and she fell to her knees. He helped her up, put his arm around her, and walked her down the stairs. He immediately left after the incident and nothing more was said.

The next time he was accosted by Elizabeth was at the annual Holiday Party. Jake brought his girlfriend to the event. She, and the other coworkers, witnessed Elizabeth's inappropriate behavior: Elizabeth sat in Jake's lap and suggestively whispered her holiday wishes to him. Understandably, this caused a fall out between Jake and his girlfriend, and this left Jake confused. Still, Jake dismissed the incident as a drunken indiscretion on Elizabeth's part.

Jake began to suspect that he was underestimating the depth of the situation when Elizabeth started asking Jake out for drinks after work. Jake thought that since they were meeting in a public place, he could keep things under control. He was embarrassed to admit that, as a man, he was in a difficult situation that was spinning out of control. His denial of the seriousness of the situation was not unusual. Over drinks, Elizabeth's conversation quickly turned personal. Jake then explained that he had a girlfriend and was unavailable for a relationship. Elizabeth did not take this well.

Soon after he told Elizabeth about his girlfriend, Jake came to the office to find that a new reporting structure had been implemented, and there was another manager between Elizabeth and himself. He knew that he had essentially been demoted. Soon afterwards, Jake received a disciplinary warning letter for being tardy. Jake protested the warning to Elizabeth; his protest fell on deaf ears. A few weeks later, he was called into Elizabeth's office and was fired. For her parting shot, Elizabeth told Jake that he did not know how to work well with women! That is when he came to see me.

Upon investigation, we found this was a powder keg of an embarrassing situation for the company, with facts more lascivious than the juiciest romance novel. The case never saw the inside of a courtroom.

What Jake should have done:

- As soon as Elizabeth displayed conduct that was unprofessional or sexual in nature, Jake should have voiced his complaint. At the very least, Jake should have reported her advances and predatory conduct to human resources and made a formal written charge of sexual harassment. The company would then have investigated the charge and taken action to stop the illegal conduct. If the company did nothing, then Jake should have taken it to an attorney.

- In making his report, Jake should have made sure to identify all the other employees who witnessed the events, especially at the holiday party. He should have maintained a careful journal of the events so that he could recount them accurately for the purpose of any in-house investigation or subsequent litigation.

- Failing to report incidents of sexual harassment where there is a complaint mechanism in place can result in doing harm to the victim. In particular, the company can assert an affirmative defense in any subsequent lawsuit that it was never given the chance to address and correct the harassment.

Attorney's comments:

- The company did not have a formal sexual harassment policy. If there is no policy and ongoing training to prevent sexual harassment (as was the case here), the company loses important defenses during trial and can be deemed to be tacitly condoning sexual harassment.
- Upon investigation, we found that this was not the first time that Elizabeth had sexually harassed a male coworker. Since upper management knew about Elizabeth's history and did nothing about it, they sent the message that such predatory behavior was normal. This had a chilling effect on the employees, who were forced to deal with this abuse and felt that any protest would likely be ignored.
- Many a times, coworkers do not report incidents of illegal behavior because they feel that the corporation

has a culture of tolerance. Their thinking is, What do I gain by reporting the incident? I am the one who will be punished. Such retribution by an employer is another type of illegal conduct called "retaliation."

Applying the lessons learned to your company:

- It is essential that you have a formal sexual harassment policy in place at your company, with several options that employees can utilize to report abuses (i.e., reporting to human resources, an ethics committee, taking legal action, etc.). Having a sexual harassment policy in place provides the company with an important affirmative defense that can help when sexual harassment charges are raised.
- Hold sexual harassment training classes on a regular basis, at least annually and at new hire orientation. If training is conducted on a regular basis, then the message from the top is that the company does not condone sexual harassment, and any such action by an individual employee is against the company.
- Encourage people to report all incidents of sexual harassment, and assure them of appropriate confidentiality.
- Investigate all reports of harassment according to your formal policy, even those that you think may be baseless.
- Do not retaliate against employees for filing sexual

harassment complaints made in good faith, even if your investigation eventually clears the alleged wrongdoer.

17.

MY EMPLOYEE WAS IN THE WRONG JOB
Steve Jordan

I was a new manager at IBM, working on the West Coast. My predecessor had been promoted and I had inherited his team, but neither the outgoing manager nor my current boss colored my thinking about my team members. They let me formulate my own decisions. My predecessor had hired Mark (name changed) from another company. He had a masters in electrical engineering and wanted to work for IBM.

The salesperson in my team sold a contract that called for the installation of computer and electronic equipment, and Mark seemed perfect for the job. I met with the client and sang Mark's praises. However, after he began working, there was one problem after another. I started getting complaints from the customer. Mark was not doing what was necessary. The documentation was not there. The computers were not operating properly. The electronics were not connected right. The salesperson was also getting complaints. I had an angry, unhappy customer who was ready to terminate our contract if I did not get someone who could perform. Mark was failing. He just could not do the job.

I put Mark into IBM's Improvement Plan. This is a ninety-day, step-by-step, detailed performance plan to get unsatisfactory work back to satisfactory performance. Despite this plan, Mark was not making progress.

He was an electrical engineer who was probably better at designing circuits than interacting with people.

It struck me that Mark was not suited to this type of work. He was an electrical engineer who was probably better at designing circuits than interacting with people. After all, he had done an excellent job for his previous employer. Mark was not good at software and systems work. He was more of an introvert and did not like to talk with people. Systems work required that he be more of a people person.

I had to help him see what he was good at and what he was not good at. My strategy was to convince him that he needed to get back into electrical engineering or he would lose those skills. I was successful in these discussions. I knew that I had to fire Mark because of his performance. Mark also knew that he was going to be fired because he was not progressing through the ninety-day improvement plan.

Mark and I both realized that this type of work was not for him. As a result, we parted amicably and Mark got a job utilizing his mechanical strengths.

What I learned:

- You need to be sensitive to the self-esteem of the person you are going to terminate. Show him a light at the end of the tunnel, and an alternative if he is talented but just does not fit in your area.
- Try to suggest a new career path and point him in a new direction, one in which you think he will succeed.

Applying the lessons learned to your company:

- If someone is not performing, you must communicate with him and tell him what is not working and give a plan to help him improve and the chance to work it out. If the person does not know that he is not performing, this discussion might shock him into improving and you have saved a career.
- Terminating an employee should be done with compassion. Prefer an amicable parting rather than a contentious one.

18.

WE HAD TO FIND A COMPROMISE
Robin Cowie
Producer, The Blair Witch Project
President, WorldWide Brands

We five were friends in a film school. After we graduated, we went our separate ways but came together to create the movie *The Blair Witch Project*. This film was the brainchild of one member of the team, Gregg Hale, who had been part of the Special Forces. Part of Gregg's training was a simulation of a prisoner-of-war environment where he was subjected to sleep deprivation, lack of food and water, and abuse. After this experience, he thought that this might be a good test for actors too.

The original script called for *The Blair Witch Project* to be divided in two segments: the Experiment and a traditional documentary. The Experiment was intended to be a unique acting and story-telling experience in Seneca State Park in Maryland. This was difficult to script and also required that we teach the actors how to use cameras and have them improvise the entire time. We gave them a Global Positioning System (GPS) and told them to go from point to point. They never knew whether the people they met were real or not. During the experiment, we moved their tents for them and had baskets where they could drop off film and get batteries. One of the directors in our team reviewed footage while the other observed. And yes, they did get lost; they were short on food, and they did get cold, all of which was captured on film.

The traditional documentary was created after the Experiment. We forged historical documents about the witch, created a news set for reports, and searched for the kids. This was the "traditional" part of the film.

When the filming was completed we had the huge task of editing the footage. The first assembled edit of the film was four hours long! That was when the challenges really began.

We needed to combine two completely different kinds of film making. The five people on the team were basically split down the middle between the traditional documentary content being combined with the experimental footage or simply going with the experimental footage as the basis of the movie.

Over the next five days we debated. We argued. We shouted. We could not agree on what to do.

As the producer, I was concerned about the financial outcome of the movie. I was not eager to throw away more than half the content we had created that cost us a large percentage of the budget.

The problem was that the Experiment portion of the project was much rougher for the audience. It was shaky, with breaks in the story, and due to the method that was used to create the footage, there was no way to answer lingering questions or recreate segments. This was a visual experience that no one had presented before. It was risky.

Over the next five days we debated. We argued. We shouted. We could not agree on what to do. We were stuck. Everyone had his valid points and insight into the right way to do it. There had to be a con-

In retrospect, the director's laying out their separate visions was the best thing that could have happened.

sensus to move forward, but we could not reach one. No one knew how to break this frustrating deadlock.

One of the directors got so mad that he came in late one night and made his own version of the film. He showed it to us the next day. The other director, not to be outdone, created his version of the film. We watched that one too. We now had two film versions with diametrically opposed points of view on how the final film should look. In addition, we had two opposite versions of the critical opening ten minutes where we had to establish the story and connect with the audience. We could not agree and we had to get the film done.

In retrospect, the director's laying out their separate visions was the best thing that could have happened. We agreed that the opening of the traditional documentary was more succinct. However, the experimental film was better overall. How could we establish the story in the experimental film? A compromise was finally reached with the question, Why not tell the audience the premise? Why not put up a card that says, "In October, 1994 three film makers got lost in the woods. A year later their footage was found?"

The light bulb went off. We had found the solution everyone could agree on. The title card was the solution to starting the film. It was amazing what that little card did to break the deadlock.

What I learned:

- Your first idea is not necessarily the best idea. Keep going, even if it means arguing.
- There were five days of difficult, emotional brainstorming. We all stood on our issues until that title card idea brought us together.
- The traditional documentary footage did not go to waste. It became the content for our now famous website www.blairwitch.com. We found a different outlet so that the brilliant ideas we just could not use in the film did not get wasted.

Applying the lessons learned to your company:

- Do not give up when you meet the first obstacle. Many a time there will be heated discussions. As long as there is trust, even with differing opinions, you know that you can keep at it until you reach a solution.

- Make sure that you are not so tied to your ideas that you cannot see a better solution. Be able to work toward compromise.

19.

I CAUGHT THE PROBLEM AT "POINT EASY"
Susan Weems
Venture Management

I have always believed in giving back and volunteered to mentor the executive director of a nonprofit outreach organization. I approached my volunteer activities by looking at the organization as a business and began to coach the Executive Director Alice (name changed). Soon I was recruited to facilitate the annual planning meeting of the nonprofit's board of directors. The board consisted of twenty dedicated, tireless, passionate community leaders.

The chairperson of the board of directors, Jean (name changed), is a dynamo. She has five children, works tirelessly for a religious organization, leads multiple volunteer groups, and continuously drives programs and people.

Alice and Jean are peers, though Alice had been a manager but had never led or built an organization. At the board's planning meeting, I saw Alice and Jean interacting with their key volunteers and supporters for the first time. They clearly operated with two vastly different styles and clashed on how to handle things.

After the meeting, I got a call from Jean. She wanted me to meet with her and another board member. They both complained about Alice. They described many instances where Alice lost her temper and argued openly with Jean in front of the volunteers and clients. Jean did not want her to quit, but she did not want her to continue acting that way either.

I met with Alice. Her position was that Jean was impossible to work with. She explained that Jean is a driver who never stops and interrupts. Alice worked constantly with additional duties and criticism. I sensed that she was angry and frustrated. This conflict had to be resolved before it created a situation that could tear apart the board and the nonprofit organization.

I asked Alice what kinds of things she could do instead of reacting in anger to what was occurring in the office.

Fortunately, the conflict was still at "Point Easy." I could help here. First, I went through my four Point Easy steps with Alice:

1. State reality unemotionally. Just tell what the situation is.
2. State how you feel, not what you feel like.
3. Recognize your contribution to the problem.

4. State clearly and unemotionally what you want.

I asked Alice what kinds of things she could do instead of reacting in anger to what was occurring in the office. The reality was that Alice and Jean could not talk civilly. Their relationship was damaged and they could not communicate (Step 1). There was a sense of loss and hurt (Step 2). Alice admitted that she contributed to the problem by her words, "She flew off the handle" (Step 3). Alice wanted to get back to working together on equal terms. She wanted to collaborate instead of fighting in front of others. Alice wanted to get back to serving the vision of the organization and helping people in need (Step 4).

Alice arranged a meeting with Jean. They met privately together and talked through these points. The conversation went on well. A new and deeper communication developed between the two women. They could then be much more focused and work together even more effectively than before. The conflict was resolved, the organization was back on track, and people are getting the services they need.

What I learned:

- Conflict resolution strategies can work in any situation where two people are not communicating, whether it is corporate, nonprofit, or family situations.

- The most difficult thing to get arguing parties to do is unemotionally state what the reality of their situation is. Sometimes it takes asking that question two or three times to get to the bottom of what is actually occurring.

Applying the lessons learned to your company:

- When conflicts arise, it is much better to resolve them before they blow up into a full blown crisis. Address them immediately. If you are still at Point Easy, follow the four steps in the story. Make sure that everyone answers question one unemotionally and factually. That is the key to resolving the issue.
- Two people who were in conflict can continue to work together successfully after clear, honest communication is established and the issues are resolved.

20.

HOW I MANAGED A GLOBAL OPERATION
George D. Wells
www.dreaminakilt.com

As an executive vice president for Fairchild Semiconductor Corporation, I had responsibility for global operations. I learned quickly that I had to choose competent, trusted managers since I could not be everywhere in the world at one time. At most I could visit each plant three times a year, but I made sure to visit all the plants at least once a year.

I charged each manager with increasing productivity, decreasing expenses, and, generally, ensuring that their plant was profitable.

I charged each manager with increasing productivity, decreasing expenses, and, generally, ensuring that their plant was profitable.

They were free to manage as they saw fit, unless there was a government issue or an asset expenditure required. I had a monthly business review with each manager. This briefing examined productivity, profitability, competition, sales and marketing, and plant conditions. I kept a pulse on what was happening in each branch around the world.

My job was made a little easier by Fairchild's policy of hiring from within wherever possible. As a result I knew many of the people that I hired before they were put in their management position. I even hired my former boss for European operations.

My plant manager in Indonesia came up with a creative solution to a productivity problem. The culture in Indonesia does not allow for confrontation. It is very hard to take a person aside and tell him he made a mistake—it crushes that person's ability to perform. Those conversations usually resulted in both quality and production going way down.

The manager was stumped at how to improve productivity without confrontation. One day he decided to put the letter A at the end of the first production row, the letter B at the end of the second production row, and the letter C at the end of the third production row. He then listed the number of units each worker made the day before under A, B, or C depending on the number of units produced and the quality of those units.

The next day the employees saw the listing when they started their shift. They were expecting an explanation. None came. The manager never said a word about the listings, just continued to post them every day. Soon all of the employees wanted to become an A— they saw that As got better raises. The manager had found

Set the ground rules and let the managers manage.

a nice way to deal with a cultural issue and improve productivity in the plant.

The Indonesia plant story is an example of my management style: set the ground rules and let the managers manage.

What I learned:

There are six things you must do to manage a global operation:
- Establish good communication. The managers must speak English to avoid translation misunderstandings.

It is critical to be clearly and consistently updated on what is happening in each plant.

- Pick managers who have experience.
- Make contact early with the governments in each country. Try to get as many training grants and tax breaks as you can before you enter the country.
- Study the local population. See whether there are universities who can teach employees.
- Have the confidence to let go. Empower your management teams and trust them to make the right decisions.
- Have good transportation to and from the plant. You must be able to get raw materials in and product out. If transportation by air becomes impossible because of weather or a strike, think of other alternatives.

Applying the lessons learned to your company:

- Hiring from within can be a great option, since you have already worked with the potential manager. You know his work style and ethics and whether you can trust him without your supervision.
- Make sure lines of communication are open. Each manager needs to understand clear boundaries: he needs to know how he will be judged as well as when he needs a higher manager's approval before taking an action.

21.

I TAUGHT CUSTOMER SERVICE TO GRUNTING TEENAGERS

Joanie Winberg
www.HappyWednesday.com

My ex-husband and I owned a True Value Hardware store in Plymouth, Massachusetts. We needed raw strength to restock shelves, lift boxes, and carry packages for our customers. Who better than teenage males?

We put the word out that we were looking for part-time help. Because Plymouth was a small town, the news spread quickly and many teenagers applied. We knew that managing them was going to be a challenge, but felt that it was worth it since we would be giving a lot of these kids their first job and starting them on the path to adulthood. We taught them service and how to be polite with people, skills that would be applicable in any job they would ever hold.

> *We taught them service and how to be polite with people, skills that would be applicable in any job they would ever hold.*

One day, John (name changed) was restocking a shelf when a customer asked him whether our store carried a particular item. He grunted an answer and the customer walked away. I was in the next aisle and heard the exchange. I quickly went to the customer and asked how I could help her. She got the item she was looking for, paid for it, and left the store.

I went back to John and explained why his response was not appropriate. I calmly explained that we cannot afford to have someone walk out of the store. It was okay if he did not know the answer, but he was expected to say to the customer, "Let me get someone to help you." Never be afraid to ask.

I tried to explain how we work with customers and advised him to be gentle and just talk with them. John listened and did not say much.

Questions went through my mind. Did John really care? Was he lazy? Did he just not want to be bothered? If his attitude did not change, I would have to let him go. I hoped that what I said to him sunk in.

Watching him over the next few days, I saw that John had heard and understood. If he did not have the answer a customer needed, he asked for help. His efforts at conversing with customers improved. I knew that he had learned an important customer service lesson.

My ex-husband still owns the True Value Hardware store and continues to hire teenagers today. In the past twenty-five years we have helped very many teenagers become productive adults. I continue to develop and use the lessons I taught the teenagers in my consulting practice. Those basic lessons form the groundwork for great corporate communications.

What I learned:

- Managing teenagers can be difficult and requires patience. You cannot yell at them or raise your voice if you want to be listened to. If you cannot get through to them about the behavioral changes they need to make after a few conversations, you need to let them go.
- We were right in our decision to hire teenagers. There were only a few that we had to let go in all the years we ran the store. Most had a good experience and gained skills that they could not learn in school.

Applying the lessons learned to your company:

- If teenagers are the right employees that you need, realize that you must be patient since this is probably their first job. They do not know what to expect, so give clear instructions regarding behavior.
- If you see an employee doing something wrong, correct the behavior immediately while it is fresh in both of your minds. A conversation a week or even two days later will not be as effective.

22.

MY DIRECT REPORTS WERE FIGHTING
Charlie Bitzis
President, Rock River Solutions

I was a new supervisor with the Delta Air Lines during the time they acquired Pan Am. I was appointed to a team of flight attendant crew scheduling analysts. This team comprised of existing Delta personnel and people who had recently joined the company as a result of the acquisition.

Most of my team fit together extremely well. We worked hard to solve the challenges resulting from the acquisition. Unfortunately, there were two people in my team who did not work well together. The first person, Jake (name changed), had been with Delta for most of his career. He felt that he was the senior member of the team and should be treated as such. The other person, Sandra (name changed), had recently joined the team after spending over twenty-five years with Pam Am. Sandra, too, felt she was the senior person. I was the new supervisor and neither respected me or my directions to our team.

Both Jake and Sandra seemed to take pride in arguing over every point and neither would accept compromise where the other was concerned. It was a very frustrating situation. I could not get them to work together. It began causing friction among the other members of the team. I realized that if I did not do something immediately, we would not get anything done.

I turned to my manager, Joanne (name changed), for help. I explained to Joanne what had been going on for several weeks and how I had tried to make Jake and Sandra respect each other's opinions. I explained that I had been ignored. I needed her help and she agreed.

Joanne handled the situation decisively and with a lesson that I apply to this day. She called both Jake and Sandra in to her office. She had me sit and watch. Joanne asked both parties what was going on. Even here, they both blamed the other and were at each other's throats.

> *She made it very clear that they would both succeed and continue their careers at Delta or they would both fail and lose their jobs.*

After listening for about five minutes, Joanne explained to both parties that they could continue to squabble if they wished. She then stated that they needed to understand that they get to decide whether or not they were going to be winners or losers in their jobs at Delta.

Joanne stated emphatically that there would either be two winners or two losers. She made it very clear that they would both succeed and continue their careers at Delta or they would both fail and lose their jobs.

Jake and Sandra got the message immediately. The turn-around in their behavior was instantaneous and dramatic.

Both learned to work with each other, the rest of the team, and me. They kept their jobs.

What I learned:

- When two (or more) talented people cannot find common ground on their own, they need to understand that management will not choose sides. Inappropriate behavior that does not work toward the goal of the organization will not be tolerated by anyone. The warring factions will suffer the consequences of their actions. There can be either winners or losers in these situations, not one of each.
- I recognized the situation was not working and I was too inexperienced to handle it. Fortunately, I had a good relationship with my boss who offered to show me how to resolve it. I never had to ask again. I learned the lesson.

Applying the lessons learned to your company:

- Conflict between two members belonging to the same team at any level of an organization can lead to disaster. This applies at all levels within an organization.
- If you see a new manager who is having issues resolving conflicts, step in to help. The manager appreciates it (and hopefully learns from it) as do the rest of the team members.

Note: I used Joanne's lesson successfully very recently. I was working with the senior management team of a retirement planning organization. Everyone's performance was evaluated individually, so each person worked toward their own success and not that of the company. They only worked to make themselves look good, which often made their counterparts look bad. On my advice, the head of marketing changed the way his employees were evaluated so that the overall marketing organization would be measured on its effectiveness, not solely on individual departmental performance. She clearly stated that they would all either succeed together or fail together. Again, the response was immediate and the teamwork that ensued was amazing.

23.

I FIRED A DRUNK
Anonymous

Our company needed a person to handle the early morning preparation activities for our company. This person had to start at 5:00 a.m. and do certain tasks so that the people who came at 6:00 a.m. could immediately get to work.

I hired a person, George (name changed), who had the experience, even though he was in his twenties, to handle the work. The normal background checks were done and during his first few weeks, George's work was great and he was able to get everything accomplished so that the people starting at 6:00 a.m. could be productive, too. Initially I was happy with his work.

Within a few weeks we began noticing some issues. Several times he was late, which caused havoc with our production and other employees' work. There was always an excuse: my baby was sick, I was out of town, and other things that seemed plausible.

During the same time the company installed an alarm system which recorded when anyone entered or exited the building. I began to see a pattern of lateness. George was so good at his job that even being fifteen or twenty minutes late usually didn't cause a problem for others, but it was still troublesome.

George was so good at his job that even being fifteen or twenty minutes late usually didn't cause a problem for others, but it was still troublesome.

The first time he was forty-five minutes late, I talked with him. Again, there was a plausible excuse. I told him that he had to call me the evening before if he was going to be late or unavailable so that I could get someone in to do his job. He abided by this for a few weeks. However, according to the time stamp on the alarm system, he was still frequently late coming to work. The unfortunate part was that when he showed up he did great work.

When his ninety-day probation period was up and his review was due, I told him (and wrote in the review) that until the tardiness improved he was not going to be hired permanently and that there would be another review in ninety days to gauge performance.

Then, one day he neither showed up for work nor did he call. This was getting serious. I wrote him up according to our procedures. I told him this was his verbal warning. Next would be a written warning and if he were late again, he would be fired. Again, there was improvement for a few days.

After this second warning, one of our other employees was moving to another state. We had a farewell dinner for her at a nearby restaurant and George and his wife came. George had too many drinks. The owner of my company instantly realized that George was an alcoholic. He was late for work the day after the dinner, again with an excuse. Unfortunately, the written warning, which he had signed, was already in place.

I couldn't sit him down and say, "George, you are ruining your life. You have a six-month-old baby. Get some help." I had to fire him. It was a sad day.

What I learned:

- Same excuses after a certain period does not make sense. You need to get to the root of the problem.
- If your company policy allows it, repeat the ninety-day

review before hiring permanently if you have doubts about the employee. At that time, we knew that George's work was good; he was just unreliable at times. However, his work in the first ninety days was not good enough to become a permanent employee at will. Therefore, I wanted to give George another ninety days before I made a decision.

- Even though I finally knew what was going on, I could not fire him for that reason. He had to be late. The underlying reason was immaterial.

Applying the lessons learned to your business:

- Larger companies may have a formal policy on alcohol and drug addictions in place. Make sure you follow those rules and policies.
- Even if you have a good employee who does good work, if he does not follow the policies, he must be fired.

24.

I MANAGE STRONG-WILLED ENTREPRENEURS ... AND LISTEN TO THEM
Rick Ritter
Idaho TechConnect, Inc.

My partner, John Glerum, and I run an incubator for start-up companies. In the past three years, we have had contact with over four hundred entrepreneurs and currently have twenty-six companies housed in the incubator. Managing these fledgling companies and their strong-willed yet sometimes naïve owners can be challenging. They all have great ideas and have strong products or services but have no clue how to start and run a business. They begin with incredible optimism but often are shocked and dismayed as the realities of business set in.

Our job is to manage their expectations and help them succeed in their businesses. John and I have found that the best thing that we can do is to be excellent listeners. The companies always had access to John, me, and our more than eighty years combined wisdom running small and large businesses. Any one of the twenty-six company presidents can drop in, sit across our desks, and try to work through their problems. We found that by simply asking questions and listening, they find the answers to their problems themselves most of the time. One of our favorite questions: What are the consequences of doing that?

By listening we become an extension of their brain; often, they will find the solutions to their problems on their own if they just talk through it. After one or two hours they usually have an epiphany.

We also find that engineers are famous for tweaking "just one more thing" before they take a product to market—

Often, they will find the solutions to their problems on their own if they just talk through it.

they have a tendency to get so wrapped up in the details that they blow deadlines. We have to make them get the product out there. This means no more changes for six months to one year. They always have an excuse why a product is not ready to ship, but we have to act as their task masters.

One of our usual warnings is that entering into a 1/3–1/3–1/3 partnership is a train wreck waiting to happen. This happened with one of the companies in the incubator. In fact, this company got the award at the end of the year for taking the most time with John and me.

Three friends who worked for a Fortune 500 technology company started their own business. One of the three took an early retirement package and was marketing the product they developed full time; the other two were still with the technology company.

They secured financing to get themselves started. All of the sales, marketing, and operations work fell to the one partner who was working on the business full time. After a while he felt resentful because he was putting in all the work without getting paid more than the others and without an increase in equity. The other two partners felt that since they had contributed the engineering expertise to get the product into a test, they were entitled to an equal amount of equity. This was an impasse that was never resolved.

The partner working full time spent hours in John's office getting motivated again whenever he felt like quitting. John listened a lot and tried to help. He did for a while. Eventually after two and a half years this partner quit working on the business full time and started with another company. The product is still available, but no one is working full time on it. By listening and asking questions John helped the frustrated partner determine what was best for him.

What I learned:

- The key to managing is listening. Many a times, just by giving these entrepreneurs an opportunity to verbally work out their problems helps them discover the answers for themselves.
- Even though we probably know the answers to all the questions that these entrepreneurs ask, the best way for them to learn is by asking questions and letting them discover the answers on their own.

Applying the lessons learned to your company:

- Managers can help their team members solve their own problems by listening and questioning. If they are stuck and cannot figure out how to resolve an issue you might give them some suggestions, but the best way to learn is for that manager to discover the solution for himself.
- Learn to question rather than immediately giving an answer when managers or employees ask you what they should do. They will learn to think on their own and come to you with potential solutions rather than just questions.

25.

HIS SALES MASKED THE PEOPLE PROBLEM
Anonymous

The state of Wyoming used to have a program where it invested in Wyoming-based businesses. The goal was to increase employment and keep industry in the state, which has less than 400,000 people. I was one of the people hired to fix companies that got into trouble.

Jim (name changed) started his company because he had to drive to Denver to get his Macintosh computer fixed. He decided there had to be a better way, so he started a mail order peripheral company in his garage. He was successful and soon grew out of his garage and into a real office. His company became the largest employer in a small town in southwest Wyoming, employing 280 people. The problem was that he could not find competent, experienced managers to control his exponentially growing company. No one had the skills he needed. As a result, he compromised and found the best people he could: a former bank teller was the CFO; a man who owned a bike shop was the Sales Manager. Neither were the right people to do the job.

Jim knew he had problems getting the right people and hired a search firm to find competent managers. He desperately needed help with his company—it experienced an average of sixty percent growth per year, eventually growing to $45,000,000 in revenues. The horse was running wild without reigns. It was out of control.

The problem was that he could not find competent, experienced managers to control his exponentially growing company.

Jim knew he was not the right manager, but the revenues and resulting accolades were blinding his judgment.

His search firm came up empty. He knew his CFO and other managers could not handle the growth situation. He did not look outside the box and try to come up with a creative solution; after all, his company had grown successfully and revenues were great. Why should he continue to try?

No one had the experience to recognize that a severe, crippling cash crunch was looming as a result of this exponential growth.

I was called upon to help when the state stepped in to offer a guarantee for the company's loans and, hopefully, survival. One of the serious issues I immediately recognized and the CFO did not have the experience to know about was that the company never had much equity. The severe cash crunch could have been avoided by obtaining equity financing rather than the debt financing that the CFO had implemented.

It was also obvious to me that, despite the lack of equity, the management team was the issue that was breaking up the company. I strongly suggested that Jim move the company. I knew that if he moved to Laramie or Cheyenne or even outside the state to Salt Lake City or Denver the company would survive. The state of Wyoming was in the game too. I thought I could convince them that to save their investment the company had to move, even if it was out of state.

Jim admitted that the current managers could not do their jobs, and no one with the right qualifications wanted to come to this small town. I tried to show him that the company had to go where competent management teams were. Jim refused even though he finally admitted the company was sinking. As a result of this inability to make the bold and right management decision, I could not help Jim. The company went out of business.

Not only 280 people lost their jobs, the state of Wyoming lost their investment.

What I learned:

- If you are not in the right place to grow, you will die. You have to find competent managers who have experience to guide people, products, and customers. If people will not come to your location, you have to go where people are.
- Sales can mask the people problem. For a long time there was cash. Even though the people could not perform their jobs, growth masked the problems. And, it distracted Jim from the real issue.

Applying the lessons learned to your company:

- Having competent managers who can handle growth is critical for survival. Before you hire a manager for a rapidly growing company, make sure he has successfully handled similar situations.
- The most critical person to find is the CFO, who handles the cash on a day-to-day basis. This person must be strong enough to scream when your company is outgrowing cash. This person must also be respected by the others on the management team. Without respect, even dire warnings will not help.
- Tough decisions need to be made to keep a growing

business in the black. If people are the problem you have got to go where the right people are for the business to survive.

26.

ASK THEM THE RIGHT QUESTIONS
Kathryn Whitecotton
Air Treatment Company

Hiring in our industry is tough. We need people who are willing to work hard to take care of our customers. Our installation crews perform manual labor all day. Many times they are exposed to extreme heat in attics or frigid cold outside or are crawling through basements. The interview process is tricky. I have to ensure that the people I hire will do good work for our customers so that we keep our stellar reputation in the community.

I have hired some nightmares. My worst was an installation helper that I did not read correctly. He made it through the interview process and drug test. After five days on the job he just freaked out and went ballistic. He stripped off his clothes! Since he was getting violent I turned to my best man on staff and had this employee immediately escorted off our property.

It has taken me a few years to get it right. Now and then I still pick a bad apple, but having said that, I hire on character. I can teach heating and air conditioning to anyone, but I cannot teach him to be honest, trustworthy, or to

> *I can teach heating and air conditioning to anyone, but I cannot teach him to be honest, trustworthy, or to have a pattern of behavior found in a morally strong person.*

have a pattern of behavior found in a morally strong person. This is really what I am looking for. People who have these traits are more likely to be team players—willing to learn, contribute, and help.

I find the right people by asking the right interview questions:

1. I always ask about hobbies. I want to know what interests them outside of work. They will start talking about what they like to do and do not like to do, which says a lot about a person.

2. I usually ask if they like to go on picnics. I know that asking about family situations is a no-no. However, they will usually volunteer things about their family when I ask this question.

3. The question that gets most of them is, did you like school? Since these are people looking for manual labor jobs, the answer is usually "No." However, I want to find out why they did not like school and if there was any part of it (other than lunch) that they did like.

4. Another revealing question is, why did you choose this industry? If they say, "For the money," I will

usually steer clear of them. If they give me other answers such as, "I like fixing things," I will see whether that matches with the answer to the hobby question. I also sense if someone is lying here.

5. Another good question, Why do you want to join our team? tells me if they know anything about our company. Most have heard something about us since we have been in business since 1958.

Finally, if the person does not have any questions for me, I get suspicious. They should ask about the working hours, overtime, benefits, and so on.

I end each interview stating that our company's reputation is not for sale. I will not put up with anything relating to dishonesty with our customers or our other employees. We are a team, we try to have fun, and we always do things in the best interest of our customers. If we do not have our reputation to stand on, we do not have a company for long.

These interview questions have helped me choose the right people for Air Treatment. Of course, I still occasionally make mistakes, and I deal with them on a case-by-case basis.

What I learned:

- Occasionally I will still have what I thought would be a good hire turn bad. In these cases I share with them the Air Treatment Way, which is also covered at the time they are hired. It is also reviewed weekly. I explain what I expect to see happen over the next couple of days. If I feel they do not understand our way after two weeks or so, I meet with them and tell them I made a mistake, and the best thing for both parties would be to part ways. I usually pay them for the pay period and give them ideas on what they should look for in another company. I also put everything in writing.

- I review the Air Treatment strategy with company employees every month. I have found that constant reminders are critical so that everyone stays on course and understands that our reputation is not for sale.

- If a good employee suddenly changes behavior or does something out of character, I relax my "boss" hat slightly and try to be a friend and find out what is going on. I tell that person I am concerned about his performance and want to know if there is anything I can help with. Most of the time, he unloads. Sometimes he shoots himself in the foot, and I make an immediate decision to end the relationship. Hostages are of no use to anyone. I stop talking and *listen*—most people just want to be heard. Most of the time, it works out and we get back to work. We are in the human relations business period. My philosophy is to lead people, manage things.

Applying the lessons learned to your company:

- Have a list of questions that you ask every interviewee. This way you can compare the answers you receive to all your questions.
- People want to be heard. Be considerate with them. Listen to what they say. This will help you manage their behavior more effectively.

27.

ENCOURAGING COMPETITION GOT ME RESULTS
Susan Harlan

I have always loved working with numbers and manipulating data. It is like working on a puzzle which, on completion, tells me about productivity, revenues, and costs. In addition, I have always found a way to help non-accounting people understand what their budgets tell them so they can see how those numbers can work for them rather than against them. By patiently explaining these "magical numbers" I can usually gain the confidence of the managers and be a part of their team.

I was working on a big project with a hospital, trying to find a way to cut costs and make those cuts acceptable to the doctors on staff who make the referrals that generate revenues for the hospital. I looked at each patient's diagnosis as a job. Each job had a revenue and a cost. What were the differences?

Calculating these job cost numbers was complex because I had to manipulate the data from different computer systems and pull it from different departments. Each department tried to resist giving me the data. However, the operations manager for the hospital understood and approved what I was doing. I had his support and the department managers begrudgingly gave me what I needed.

I found that for the same diagnosis (i.e., job) one job cost might be $30,000 more than another job cost. We had to find a way to reduce all costs to those lowest costs for that job rather than the highest. That required talking with the doctors.

We thought of a plan which revolved around, "The more you save, the more commission you get". When we presented it to the doctors they hated it. We implemented it anyway. Upon investigation a few months later, we found that they started charging more so they could save more and thus make more commission. This obviously was not working.

What we did see was that the doctors were competitive with each other. I created a report for each diagnosis (job). Doctors' names were listed as A, B, C, and so on. The cost was listed next to each letter. Then we discussed the report privately with each doctor. We said, for example, "You are Doctor A with a cost of $25,000 for this diagnosis. Most of the other doctors, as you can see, are at $10,000. What can you do about it?"

First, the higher costing doctors said that they had sicker patients. We showed them that it was not true. Then they said that the other doctors just forgot to document costs. They had to

> *The peer pressure made the costs come down.*

do the documentation for billing (and they knew it), so this was not true either.

Even though names were not listed, the higher cost doctors knew who the lower cost doctors were and began talking with them about how they managed their care of a certain diagnosis. The peer pressure made the costs come down. Soon everyone was in line with the lower diagnosis (job) costs. The operations manager loved the results as did the doctors who truly wanted efficiency.

What I learned:

- It took an operations person to enforce giving me the information I needed to evaluate costs. The departments were like fiefdoms. Each had their own turf and did not want anyone intruding on it.
- By breaking everything down into simple units, that is, referring to diagnoses as "jobs," I could evaluate revenues and costs using a standard measurement.

This allowed me to compare everything fairly and massage the data to see what was really happening.

- Competition between peers often brings the results that you want. No one wants to be the odd man out. Everyone will strive to be the best when everyone is evaluated the same way and they understand the way that they are being evaluated.

Applying the lessons learned to your company:

- Forcing two departments to share information usually results in everyone having a better understanding of the whole picture. If you are the operations manager find a way that the groups become willing to share for the good of the company.
- Break a complex issue into units that can be measured. This way you can compare all aspects of the issue fairly and evenly.

28.

I FIRED MY STAR EMPLOYEE
Anonymous

I was hired by the owner of a small company to build the service department. One of my first jobs as service manager was to assess the technical competence of the employees working in the department. I found their skills were inadequate and realized that I needed to train them. In addition, I needed to grow the department so I started looking for skilled technicians.

After a few weeks of searching, interviewing, and testing, I found a very skilled, customer-friendly technician, Mark (name changed). I hired him. The first few weeks on the job Mark was a manager's dream come true: He did things right the first time, communicated with the customer, and generated a lot of revenues for the company.

Unfortunately, the other technicians got jealous. Instead of learning from Mark, they started resenting him. Unbeknownst to me, the technician who had been there the longest, Jim (name changed), felt the most threatened. He plotted to get rid of my new star.

Our employee manual at the time described fireable offenses. The verbiage written in the manual stated: *These are fireable offenses: Illegal drug usage, alcohol cans/bottles in a company vehicle, stealing, and moonlighting.* Jim knew the manual, as all the employees did—they were required to sign a statement agreeing to abide by the company policies. He decided to put an open beer can in Mark's truck!

Jim snuck a beer can into Mark's truck knowing that it would be discovered during one of the weekly truck checks. The following Monday I found the can. I was shocked. I could not imagine why he would drink and drive on the job; he seemed to be such a good employee.

I called Mark into my office. I showed him the beer can. Mark was shocked and denied that he had put it there. And I believed him. Unfortunately, our policy manual read: *These are fireable offenses*. So, I had to abide by the company policy at the time and fired my star employee.

> *Unfortunately, our policy manual read: These are fireable offenses.*

I knew something was wrong. I knew Mark did not drink on the job and I could not imagine him leaving the company. I dug into the situation and found that Jim had actually put the beer can in Mark's truck. I fired Jim.

Since there was no policy on when you could rehire a fired employee, I called Mark and rehired him two weeks after I fired him. Thankfully he agreed to come back. And we changed the company policy manual to read: *These may be fireable offenses*.

What I learned:

- You have to abide by the company policy no matter how much it hurts. The rules must be applied fairly to everyone.
- Company policies can be changed if situations warrant it. In this case, we changed one word to give the company some flexibility.
- I have to do a better job integrating new employees

with current employees, especially those who are technically better than current employees.

Applying the lessons learned to your company:

- Make sure that your company manual is reviewed by an attorney familiar with the employment law. The attorney will make sure that you do not get stuck with a rigid clause like the one in this story. It is worth the cost of the review.
- A new employee can cause resentment, especially if he is hired to improve a department. Make sure that you encourage other employees to learn from the new hire. Do not let resentment build up or it could destroy your department.

29.

MEDIATING FAMILY ISSUES MADE ME SICK
Norma Owen

By the time I was twenty, I was a manager in my stepfather's business and best in terms of the revenues per square foot and inventory turns. I was a twenty-year-old female beating the older, supposedly more seasoned, men. Despite my great revenues I made every management mistake that could be conceived of. I learned quickly to clearly state what I wanted and make sure that people understood what was expected of them. I got over wishing that people could read my mind. I got over being nice. I got over bad hiring mistakes. I got over allowing excuses.

Within a year I became a good manager as well as a good revenue producer. I expected follow-through. I clearly wrote what I expected. I implemented the "three strike rule" (verbal warning, written warning, firing). I developed many of the practices that I still use today in my current business, the Avadon approach.

About four years later my stepfather retired and my stepbrother took over, but it was not a clean transfer of power; in fact, it really happened in name only. There was a lot of resentment because my brother was not really running anything and the long-time managers still looked to my stepfather for direction.

Managers looked at me as the mediator and spent a lot of time taking sides rather than focusing on the things they had to do to generate revenues for the company.

There was confusion about who to take orders from and anger when managers were getting different answers from different bosses. My stepfather could not separate himself from the business and just could not bear to move out of my brother's way. And my stepbrother would not do anything to hurt his father. He did not want to be the son who threw his father out of the family business.

As a result, I got a lot closer to my stepfather. I heard his side of the story as well as that of my stepbrother's. Managers looked at me as the mediator and spent a lot of time taking sides rather than focusing on the things they had to do to generate revenues for the company. Instead of fighting the competition, they argued about who to be loyal to. The power struggle between my stepfather and stepbrother was tearing the company apart.

It was also tearing me apart. They did not talk to each other. They talked through me. I was the messenger. My mother also got involved, so I had three people talking to me, who should have been talking to each other. On top of this political mess, I was now the southern division manager running three branches and traveling three weeks per month. I had the normal management responsibilities *and* I had to mediate between my family members. Who should I listen to? The man who built the company? The man who will own the company? My mother? Eventually this stress took a toll on my health.

When my brother took over he kept all of the managers who were loyal to my stepfather. He did not hire his own team and relied on the loyalty of those managers who had been at the company for a long time. In retrospect, this might have been a mistake. However, my stepbrother was smart enough to hire one of his business professors. His professor helped him earn the respect that was necessary to take the company forward. He helped the managers focus on the business and not take sides in the personal dispute going on between my stepfather and stepbrother.

I realized that I could not salvage the situation between my stepbrother and stepfather and finally left the company. My stepbrother took the reins and runs a profitable company today. I took the management skills that I had learned and use them as the basis for the management training and process that I developed at Avadon.

What I learned:

- I had to see the company as a separate entity from me. My stepfather could not seclude himself from the company and that caused a lot of problems for my brother.
- I should have forced my stepfather and stepbrother to talk. They never got the opportunity to talk it out, lay all their issues on the table, and then reconcile. A confrontation between them would have hurt, but solved the lingering problems as well and created a resolution to the business issues.
- Managing employees is easy compared to managing family situations.
- I am a task-oriented individual by nature. I had to learn to manage the emotional side of employees, family, and mine. I got the employee management down. I never did get the family emotional management down.
- I will never again keep peace at the expense of my health.

Applying the lessons learned to your company:

- Outside mediation can be critically important in a family business. If there are succession issues and it is unclear who is in charge, non-family employees will take sides and focus on the political fight rather than operating their segment of the business. An outsider can say things family members won't say to each other and help everyone resolve the family issues so the business can survive.

- If a younger generation is assuming control, they must establish authority quickly. If there are still managers loyal to the old regime, a conversation must be had about who is in charge. In addition, the younger generation must be respected by the older generation: the older generation cannot sabotage the younger generation's management decisions.

30.

WE BOUGHT A COMPANY AND LEFT FORMER OWNERS IN PLACE
Anonymous

After selling my staffing company, I became restless and started looking for a company to buy. My neighbor was experienced in evaluating companies. She worked in mergers and acquisitions for a Fortune 500 company and had bought or sold companies with a value of more than $2 billion. She and I teamed up. I relied on her experience to find the right company and value it properly. I did not think to ask about her management style.

We found a staffing company, made an offer, and allowed the two former owners to retain forty-five percent ownership. To my surprise, I discovered that my neighbor did not do the due diligence well. Within a few weeks we learned how much trouble that company was really in. Now instead of two people, there were four people trying to manage a sinking ship. We thought that growth would cure the issues and were relying on promises from my neighbor partner's former company to provide revenues. This never materialized.

> *Anything I said could be and was disputed by a former owner or my neighbor partner.*

I also found out that I had a very different management style from my new partner and the former owners of the company. This caused havoc in the office. The twenty full-time employees of ours were bothered by the lack of consistent management. They became fractional and did not know what was going on. Anything I said could be and was disputed by a former owner or my neighbor partner. There was no consistent message given to our employees. The staff became immobile and non-productive. They still had loyalties to the former owners and were totally demoralized.

This was definitely not my management style. However, I did not have the ownership stake to do something about it. All I was doing was pouring money into a company that was going nowhere, with former owners who had managed badly and still had influence.

I quit nine months after the purchase of the company. I could not manage the staff the way I had successfully done in the past companies because I did not trust my partners. I was tired of the drama, walked away from my investment, and cut my losses.

What I learned:

- Find out how your partners think before you begin working with them. Make sure they have the same management philosophy (not necessarily the same style) and ethics that you do. Had I spent more time with my neighbor in a working environment I probably would not have invested with her.
- The employees need a consistent message from the top. One manager cannot say something totally opposite from what another has said. Mixed messages cause paralysis rather than productivity.
- Having former owners on the management team can be bad. Loyalties are still there and employees may not respect the new owners' wishes.

Applying the lessons learned to your company:

- People can have different management styles. However, they must be on the same wavelength and have a consistent message. Issues must be settled out of sight of your employees so the staff only sees management functioning as one.
- If you cannot manage effectively because of higher managers' directives or partners who cannot agree, then it might be time to quit. Life is too short to be miserable.

31.

I INHERITED AN EMPLOYEE WHO HATED ME
Anonymous

I was promoted to manager of customer service and became boss to the people who were already in the department. I had come from a different department and so was starting fresh—I had not worked with any of them before. I was very focused on getting the work done, but tried to keep the atmosphere in the office light and was available to help whenever needed.

One of the women in the department, Jane (name changed), did not like working for me. My predecessor had hired her and even though he was no longer there, she resented anyone with authority who replaced him.

Jane resisted everything I tried to do even though the changes were necessary and better for our customers. To make matters worse, Jane began a relationship with a gentleman in another department who was continually coming up to see her, taking her focus away from what little work she was doing and causing a disruption for the other people in the department.

She continually made mistakes which cost the company money. In addition, Jane was using the company's printers to print personal pictures on company time and expense. But more important, her telephone demeanor left a bad impression with some of our customers. Her retort when I brought up a comment that I had gotten from a customer: "I'm not a Barbie doll and I do not answer the phone the same way every time"

I wanted to fire her because her work was sub-par; she was disruptive, argumentative, and resisted any changes. However, I did not think it was fair to do that without trying to make the situation work. And, our policy manual required that I build a case before fir- *I told Jane that her job was on the line and that if her performance did not improve she was gone.* ing her. I began looking for a potential replacement while I prepared to talk with Jane about her work performance.

I made a list of the issues. I included paperwork she had not completed properly as well as the necessary changes in attitude. I included examples of the problems as I saw them. The discussion was incredibly difficult. I had to be straight and honest. I told Jane that her job was on the line and that if her performance did not improve she was gone. From the look on her face, she was shocked but seemed to get the message. I also told her that the visits from her boyfriend were causing a problem. They disrupted all the members of the team and took focus away from work. The visits had to stop unless it was break time or there was a work reason for him to be in our department.

At the end of the discussion I gave her a copy of my list and had her sign it. I kept a copy and put it in her personnel file. This was the greatest shock to her: the fact that I had written everything down really told her that I was serious.

I agreed to meet up with her everyday to go over paperwork. Soon the mistakes became fewer and fewer and her attitude improved dramatically. The non-business-related visits from her boyfriend became nonexistent. We still had little skirmishes for the next few months. However, they became infrequent. Within six months Jane became one of my best employees.

During her yearly evaluation this year, Jane's work earned her a reasonable raise. This sent her a message that hard work would be rewarded. I am no longer looking for her replacement.

What I learned:

- Even if you did not hire the employees you supervise, you have to try to work with the team you are managing.
- When difficult situations arise, deal with them immediately and do not let them get any worse.
- I was not sure whether Jane would stay after the written warning, so I needed to start looking for her replacement as I was preparing it.
- Difficult employees can be turned around and their performance improved dramatically.

Applying the lessons learned to your company:

- Make sure that you understand company policies. You have to build a case and follow the procedures for disciplining and firing employees. Otherwise, the policy manual is ineffective.
- Sometimes difficult employees can be turned around through direct conversations and examples of the mistakes which need to be corrected.
- Always have a back up plan if difficult conversations go awry. If Jane had quit, her replacement needed to be in place to continue smooth department operations.

32.

I PUT MY FAMILY AHEAD OF MY JOB
Ralph Quinn

At thirty-two I was working, married, and had three children. I volunteered to head a massive fund drive for my church. This involved raising millions of dollars. The priest said to me, "Be low key. Let the people unload on you." I could not believe what he said. I was a young kid talking to senior citizens with a lot of money. Why would they talk with me?

But the priest was right. They did talk to me and ended up teaching me a valuable lesson that changed the way I looked at work. Over and over again I heard people who were sixty years old with millions of dollars net worth talk about

> *Family is important because you cannot take your millions to the grave.*

returning to an empty house. Their wives had divorced them. Their kids hated them because they spent all their time building their businesses. I got the message loud and clear: Family is important because you cannot take your millions to the grave; you cannot wire transfer funds to heaven either. Even though these people had a lot of money, they were miserable. I vowed from that point on to always put my family ahead of work.

I meant it. I was the senior vice president of marketing for a company with five-thousand employees. The chairman of the board was a seventy-two-year-old farmer whose life was all about work. He reminded me of one of the men that I talked with during my church fund-raising years.

I reported updates and concerns to the board of directors at the mandatory monthly board meeting. One month there was nothing new on the agenda and there were no pressing problems. Since there was nothing earth-shattering that was going to happen, I thought that one of my managers could get some experience by attending in my place. I went to my son's soccer game.

The next day, the chairman called me into his office. He asked me why I was not at the meeting. I told him that I had reviewed the agenda prior to the meeting and knew nothing pressing was going to be discussed, and thought that sending my manager would be good experience for him. I explained that my son had a soccer game and the game was important to both of us. He did not seem pleased and I was afraid I would get fired, but if so, then so be it. I was good at what I did and could get another job. I could not get another family.

I had lunch later that week with another senior manager and related the conversation I had with the chairman. I included the fact that I thought that he was going to fire me over it. The manager said, "Are you kidding? He's been bragging all week about you. He wished that he had more men working with him with your kind of backbone."

What I learned:

- You have to stand up for what you believe in. I was willing to put my career on the line for my family. In fact, I have done it many times and have never been fired.
- I have taught this philosophy to all my employees over the years. I explain my experience with the church fund-raising drive and tell them my philosophy. Every quarter I meet with my managers to discuss the quarter's goals. We agree on four or five to be accomplished. But I also get their important dates: soccer games, dance recitals, vacations, and so on. These go on my calendar too so I can make sure that team members attend those family functions. Many times I have kicked a person out of the office at 3:00 p.m. to attend the event. If I see them working late consistently, I ask them what is so important that it could not be done the next day. If it is a presentation that they have waited until the last minute to do, I will get on their case about not starting it earlier.
- I found that I have more productive employees when they realize they can take time off for their children's and other family member's events. When they get back to the office they work harder.
- I have a wonderful relationship with my wife and children. I have had a great career and a family that cares about each other. Now I teach entrepreneurs

and other executives that, if they have not already started building a loving relationship with their wives and children, they can start it now. They do not have to come into an empty house at night when they are sixty or seventy.

Applying the lessons learned to your company:

- Make sure that you have clearly stated policies for notice of and leaving work for family functions. Define what is acceptable. Then, follow the policy.
- Lead by example! Set clearly defined family balance policies and then practice them yourself.
- Learn to enjoy your career, spend time with your spouse and family, always be proud of your actions and accomplishments. Yes, you can have your cake and eat it too!

33.

THE PRESIDENT TRIED TO BULLY ME
Anonymous

I became the executive director of a northern Chamber of Commerce. A woman, Sharon (name changed), became vice president and subsequently, the president of the chamber. She micromanaged everything and became my worst nightmare. I had not worked with non-profit boards before and I did not know what my options were or how to handle this situation.

Here is what happened: Sharon typically came into my office at least in a month, closed the door, and started yelling about little things such as a misspelling in a newsletter. She told me that the entire board was unhappy with my disorganization and lack of detail. Sharon positioned herself as the "good guy" against the "bad guy" board. She said that she was trying to help me.

I thought that Sharon represented the board's opinions—after all, she was the president. I did not want to seem as if I was complaining, so I did not say anything. I was too new and did not know what my authority was.

> *There was nothing I could say during her moments of rage that would calm her down.*

I had given Sharon a key so that she could come in early when seminars and meetings were held. One day she slipped a derogatory letter under my door, warning that I was not up to par and that my job was in jeopardy. I found out later that she did this without the board's approval.

Sharon continued to verbally assault me. There was nothing I could say during her moments of rage that would calm her down. One time she invited a board member to sit in on one of our meetings. Sharon unleashed on me again. The board member called the person he was having lunch with, and calmly told him that he was going to be late. After Sharon's tirade, he called her "General" in a sarcastic manner.

At this point I was able to talk with another board member about her outbursts. I asked him whether the board was unhappy with me. He said no. They had no idea what she was doing. They did not know about the warning letter that she had slipped under my door.

The last time I let Sharon shout at me was right before Christmas when we were going caroling with the chamber ambassadors. Sharon said that she had to see me right away even though she knew everyone had assembled. They would just have to wait. This time, the entire office and chamber members saw her behavior. It made them see what type of person she really was. Her actions turned both the staff and the chamber members against her. At this point my staff hated her.

Soon after, the entire board heard about this latest incident. They wanted to know what was actually going on and assured me that I was doing a good job. They suggested that I document each incident and send them to the board. In addition, the board members suggested that everything Sharon brought up to me should be brought up to the board in front of her. The first few times, Sharon resisted and said that it was not a board issue. I disagreed and the board backed me.

One day, I hit my breaking point. Sharon came into my office and closed the door. Before she started shouting at me, I got up, opened the door, and told her to come back when she could calmly discuss her issues. I finally got control of the situation.

What I learned:

- You do not have to take shouting and inappropriate behavior from anyone. People can discuss things as rational adults. Whenever I see irrational, emotional behavior, I ask that person to come when he or she is calmer so we can rationally discuss an issue.
- I took too much grief before I went to others on the board. Even though others said that I was doing a good job I questioned my abilities because of Sharon. I should not have waited so long.

Applying the lessons learned to your company:

- Focus on your job and the results that are expected of you. If the results are there but you are still unsure about your performance, ask your superiors what their opinions are.
- A disruptive employee or boss can cause havoc with the organization. Find a mentor who can help you through situations and keep you on track. Your mentor is critical if you want to stay with the business. Or, if the situation becomes intolerable, document the issues and go to the boss's boss. If a person

is harming your ability to work effectively, then the boss's boss should know. *It is likely you are not the first person the troublemaker has made miserable.*

34.

"WE NEED TO PART WAYS" WAS MUSIC TO MY EARS
Anonymous

I became a subcontractor to a well-known, large service company in New York. The company had a good reputation in the area and was doing well—when you looked at it from the outside.

I reported to a supervisor who told me the customers whom I had to work for and the work expected of me. In the beginning everything went smoothly. I did the work that the customers wanted. When there were problems on other company jobs I fixed them. However, the supervisor neither gave me credit for the work that I did nor thanked me for solving the customer's problems. I did not like this and felt exploited. However, I got more work from the company and got sucked in.

Other problems soon appeared. The company owner hired an employee who could do no wrong, even though it became obvious that he did not know what he was doing. I eventually found out that he was selling drugs to the company owner. No wonder the guy could do no wrong!

In addition, the morals of the company began changing. I was invited to partake in drug and porno parties. Neither interested me; I was raised with Christian values and was in the National Guard. I had absolutely no interest in those ethics or ways of life.

> *Since I was not participating in their debauchery, they assumed there had to be something wrong with me.*

That is when things began crashing down around me. Since I was not participating in their debauchery, they assumed there had to be something wrong with me. They constantly criticized my work. Even though I continued to bail out the supervisor's problems, I could do nothing right. They began spreading rumors about me in the community, which were totally untrue.

Why did I stay? I had to learn as much as I could and the constant jobs were providing the food on my table and the roof over my head. I had all of my eggs in one basket. Even though it was a rotten basket and I dreaded working there, I was trapped.

A few months after the company morals changed, the owner of the company called me into his office and said, "We have to part ways." That was one of the happiest days of my life. I use the memories of this extremely negative situation as examples of how not to treat employees.

What I learned:

- If you are in an environment of extreme, unhealthy competition based on personal relationships that appear less than professional, plan on becoming an outsider.
- Thank the people who help you fix problems. Do not take credit for someone else's accomplishments. It is lying and makes that person less likely to help in the future.
- If your entire income is dependent on what you are doing and you hate going to work, you have to find something else to generate income.
- If the business does not fit with your morals and ethics you do not belong there. You will be miserable and stressed out.
- Feedback is critical. I learned a lot about how to do my job well even though I was constantly criticized for the work I was doing. In the beginning, the negative feedback about my work was important to me because it taught me how to do things right.
- By talking to the customers I worked with, I learned what their issues were and by satisfying them, I was able to build a business. Had I not been treated so poorly I probably would have shared these with the owner of the company. However, I kept the information to myself and used it to help me.

Applying the lessons learned to your company:

- Team environments are critical to success. When it comes to winning or losing, people start competing with each other and do not work together toward the company's success. Then the company loses, the customer loses, and the employees lose.

- If you find an employee or a subcontractor who is very unhappy and is not enjoying work, find out whether you can remedy the situation. If not, the best thing for that person is to ask him to leave. It might seem harsh especially since he might be dependent on your company for all of his income. However, in the long run, the person will be much happier finding a place that he fits in, is productive, and contented.

- By listening to employees and subcontractors, you can find out the trends they are seeing with customers. This information will help you provide the goods and services that your customers want and help cement customer relationships and future business.

35.

MANAGING THE START UP OF OUR FAMILY BRAND
Paul, Hermine, Juliette, and Olivia Brindak

Miss O & Friends started because Juliette and Olivia, the children in our family, needed to express themselves and reach out to others of their age group who were experiencing the same feelings. We created a website which would serve them to communicate with their friends and their friends' friends. We wanted the girls to build a sense of self and gain self-esteem. We did not know that we were starting a huge community with over one billion hits (as of June, 2006), six books, and many licensees.

I (Paul) have started companies in the past and have worked for many corporations. I talked with Juliette's and Olivia's friends and many other teen girls on a one-on-one basis, asking about their interest in Miss O & Friends, and for their ideas for the website and for licensing applications. The response was 100 percent positive; I was stunned. In all of the product introductions I have done, I had never gotten such an overwhelming response. We bet the farm

> *The hardest thing was the time commitments of our daughters, who had to learn to manage school work, friends, and a business.*

on the idea. We took our daughters' college funds and I stopped working for others. The hardest thing was the time commitments of our daughters, who had to learn to manage school work, friends, and a business.

As the spokesperson for the business, Juliette has had mixed results. While she enjoys speaking with the media, she has missed school and the business has had an impact on her grades. I have had to go to her teachers and school counselors and explain what was going on. Some of her teachers understood that there were times that she had to miss school.

As the business picked up, I (Juliette) had less and less time. At first it was frustrating. I learned that if I sit down and focus I do better. I wanted to keep my grades up, but I wanted a life too—see my friends, watch TV, and have a social life. I had to find a way to do everything.

I had to learn not to procrastinate and for the most part I do not. Managing homework and business is hard because there is always so much to do. Now I spread things out that I have to do, whether it is a school term paper or an article that I have to write. If I do this, I'm not totally stressed out the night before thinking about getting something done.

My teachers get frustrated when I miss school. They ask me a lot about Miss O & Friends. Over the years they have learned that this is important to me. I consider the business "my sport." I do not think that it is any different from my friends who are involved in sports having to miss school. It has helped that we are a virtual company so I can get on a computer anywhere and get work done. I can focus, complete what I need to do, and even have the time for a social life too.

What we learned:

- This business is a great balancing act. Not only did we have the business issues, we had the parenting issues. As a family business with growing children, where the business was totally dependent on the children's views, we had to learn to separate the discipline of "parenting issues" from the "business issues." We make it clear which is which, and the girls respect us in both.
- Communication is the key. Letting the school know what is happening is critical to keeping Juliette and Olivia in the business. They still have to complete all the work. However, their teachers know what is happening and most have made some allowances to make up the tests and work missed.
- By learning to focus and not procrastinate, Juliette has learned management skills that will help her function well as an adult.

Applying the lessons learned to your company:

- When you have multiple tasks and seemingly little time to do them, break the tasks into *doable* segments. Even if you only have five minutes you can return a telephone call or an email.
- Focus and concentration help you get everything done. Try to get at least some time every day where you will not be interrupted.
- In family businesses you must separate family issues from business issues. In the business someone must be the boss. Be clear about communicating which is which so that family issues do not creep into the business and cause problems.

36.

GETTING THE OWNER OF A FAMILY BUSINESS TO PLAN FOR SUCCESSION
Anonymous

One of my clients, Ned (name changed), is a man in his sixties who started a business early in his life. He grew it from a one-man operation to a multi-million-dollar corporation. A little background: Ned has six children, four from his first marriage (two sons and two daughters) and two daughters from his second marriage. Of the four children from his first marriage, two sons and two sons-in-law are operating divisions of the company. His daughters were not asked, nor permitted, to be involved in the business. However, their husbands are involved. The two daughters he had with his second wife are too young to be a "factor" yet.

Ironically, Ned's right-hand person, who has been with the company since its inception, is a woman, Nancy (name changed). Now, Nancy has effectively taken over the day-to-day operations of the business. Ned handles business development and is spending more time away, leaving the details of running the business to her. Nancy hired a CFO, who saw signs that Ned wanted to retire and pushed for succession planning. Ned reluctantly agreed.

I was brought in to do the succession plan. Ned told me that he did not want to spend much time on it and to do the work with the CFO and Nancy. He was not engaged. I could tell he did not want to do this. Finally, he did make one tough decision. He determined that none of his sons or sons-in-law could take over the business when he retired. They were to continue running their individual divisions and Nancy would run the day-to-day operations, which she was essentially doing already. Since Nancy had watched his children grow up she knew them well and had earned their respect.

It was obvious to me that Ned was avoiding making most of the decisions, which, of course, only he could make.

It was obvious to me that Ned was avoiding making most of the decisions, which, of course, only he could make. He did not enjoy the process and did not want to be a part of it. Meanwhile, tensions with his second wife were mounting. She wanted to make sure that she and her daughters would be taken care of. She did not get along with her step-children. I told Ned that I needed to meet his wife. She and I developed a good relationship. During the discussions I told Ned that he could easily purchase a life insurance policy made payable to his new wife and daughters. This pleased her and solved a huge problem for Ned. Once I proposed the life insurance and his wife agreed, his problems seemed to evaporate. His wife would be taken care of outside the business and his older children would take care of and be cared for by the business: the life insurance policy killed two birds with one stone and solved Ned's problems.

Even though the daughters were not running the business, equity was divided equally among the older children. However, there was a strong operational agreement in place that despite the equity, Nancy was running the company.

What I learned:

- Sometimes it is a simple solution that allows succession issues to be resolved. In this case the life insurance policy resolved most of the issues; it evaporated the tension between his second wife and his older children and left Ned able to focus on the decisions that needed to be made for the company.

- Even though there is respect, when it comes to equity, most closely held family businesses stick together and do not award equity to outsiders.
- Succession planning is critical in all businesses. Without a plan in place for the transfer of power, employees will be confused about who to take directives from, operations could be interrupted, and the company could stall and lose profits while everything is figured out.

Applying the lessons learned to your company:

- Making succession decisions is difficult; especially when the owner realizes that no family members have the capabilities to run his company. However, these difficult decisions must be made for the business to survive.
- Once a critical decision gets made, whatever that critical decision is, the rest of the succession plan usually runs smoothly.

37.

I MADE THE TOUGH ETHICAL DECISION
Anonymous

I was hired as the president of a $200 million division of a Fortune 500 company. The division had lost about $10 million the year before I arrived. Looking at the company's financial statements before I agreed to take the position, I realized there had been few capital improvements in the plants in recent years. Usually, one looks for investment at least equal to the amount of depreciation each year. I was concerned, so I took my eighty-year-old father to our main factory because he had worked in the machine tool industry. His comment was, "Some of this machinery is older than I am!"

During the negotiations before I agreed to take on the position, the company's management had agreed to spend the investment dollars needed to upgrade the facilities and decrease production costs. They believed, at this point, that fixing this business would aid in their diversification. I signed on.

A few months after I took the job, my boss came to me and said that there was a change in the corporate thinking. The strategic decision had been made not to invest additional dollars in our plants because the company needed to spend available capital on purchasing companies in another business category.

Our CFO retired around the same time as this reverse in thinking. At his retirement party he asked me to meet him in the office the following Saturday. I agreed. He came to me with a box. In the box were the files of "balance sheet problems," known only by upper management, totaling over $10 million. I was shocked. In the face of attempting to recoup the losses caused by the labor stoppage we now had to deal with several large balance sheet discrepancies that needed to be written off the income statement. To get the company in the black we did not need $7 million on the bottom line, but now close to $20 million!

Since additional plant investment was not going to be found, there were only a few options: increase sales of our products, look into outsourcing of component production, consolidate operations in the "newer" facilities, and do some general belt-tightening in the administrative areas of the business. Increasing sales was not hard and I was successful at managing the sales team to generate the additional revenues.

The gut-wrenching piece was making the decision to close plants. I decided to close one in the northwest. This particular plant was essentially manufacturing the products with minimal automation. The products were functionally sound but the appearance was not what it needed to be. Most importantly, the plant suffered in terms of overall productivity per labor dollar. These products could be easily incorporated into the production lines by our factory in the Midwest. As a result, 180 factory workers, mostly welders and other skilled laborers, would lose their jobs.

My boss suggested I send a letter notifying the employees that the factory would close as of a specified date. I was appalled at his insensitivity and lack of business ethics. I knew that, as the leader of this team, I had to go and tell the people myself. It was my responsibility as the decision maker to do the right thing.

I flew to the plant with a couple of other management staff. On the airplane I was very anxious. There were enough concerns over the potential employee reactions that our parent company insisted on hiring two bodyguards, who met us at the hotel where the meeting was held. No one knew what was going to happen. However, I felt strongly that it was my responsibility

During the meeting I explained that to save the entire company, some divisions of the company had to be sacrificed.

to meet with these "soon to be ex-employees" and answer their questions as honestly as I could as to why this decision was made.

During the meeting I explained that to save the entire company, some divisions of the company had to be sacrificed. I offered jobs to people who were willing to move to other locations. Only 2 of the 180 moved. I answered all their questions. Some wanted explanations. Others just wanted to vent their anger and fear. The reality was the plant would close and they would have to look for other employment.

After the meeting, while feeling sad, I knew that I had done the right thing facing the employees and explaining our decision the best that I could. I was the president and I had to stand up and explain management's actions.

I turned the division around in the eighteen months I spent as president. The first year we were slightly profitable and we were on track to generate a significant profit the following year when I left the company. The hard decisions were necessary to save it.

What I learned:

- People may not like the decisions you make. However, most will accept them if you explain the reasons for your actions and are honest. Acknowledge that you do not expect them to agree with you, but that you want them to at least understand your position.
- Be direct and give bad news in person, even though it is hard. Do not hide behind a piece of paper.

Applying the lessons learned to your company:

- People are usually the key to turning around a company. With the right team in place and the right management, you can accomplish the task.
- Open and honest communication is a key requirement.

- Make the hard decision to fire people quickly. Do it at once. It is much better to let 180 people go in a day rather than laying off thirty at a time over a six-week period.

38.

I HIRED THE WRONG PERSON
Clay Nelson
Clay Nelson Life Balance

The nature of my business is such that I do not have many employees. However, the employees that I do have must be reliable and be counted on to follow the direction that I set for the business. I am a coach so I should be able to coach, correct, and help my employees succeed. Right? Wrong!

I was looking for another employee. My feeling is that if someone wants to work for me and the fit is right, I give that person every opportunity to prove herself. Mary (name changed) came to me wanting to work with our company. I looked at her résumé. It fit my needs. I checked out her references. They said that she could do the job that I needed accomplished. She appeared to be a go-getter and exactly what I needed.

During the interview process, she said that there were some things that she could do well and ideas that she wanted to implement. I would come to find out that she did do *some* things really well, but there were many, many other things she did not do well at all.

Over a period of six months it became clear that she did not have the skills or the drive she spoke of. I thought, "I am a coach. I can handle this situation and change Mary's behavior and drive." I did not want to fire her; I was determined to change her into the employee I wanted and kept giving her more and more chances to learn from her mistakes. I wanted to set an example for my clients.

> *If I had been coaching a client with someone like Mary as an employee, my recommendation would have been to let her go long before I did.*

It was one catastrophe after the other (admittedly, piled in between the things she did well). We had numerous conversations to try to correct her actions. I saw that Mary was a gifted person in several areas, but in the end I thought her rather toxic way of communicating got in the way of her ability to perform at her greatest potential.

The painful truth was she did not want to make a difference with our company. If I had been coaching a client with someone like Mary as an employee, my recommendation would have been to let her go long before I did. Why did I have such a problem seeing clearly with my own company and my employees?

Mary was shocked when I let her go. She thought that she had been doing a great job. It was difficult for her to understand why she was fired. I explained the best that I could. I showed her no animosity, but made it clear that where she was trying to take the company was a direction that I thought I had clearly stated I did not want to go. This was causing havoc with my clients and me, and I had to find a person who could follow the path I had set.

The next person I hired is doing well. And, I am much more objective about her work than I was with Mary. In hindsight, I realized that it took me too long to make the change. I could not alter the behavior of someone who did not want to be what I needed. This is a mistake which should not happen again.

What I learned:

- I have much more empathy for what my clients are going through—it is difficult and painful to make the decision to fire someone.
- No matter how much I want to make a difference, not everyone wants to have a difference made. When someone shows signs of not wanting to change, I have to admit it and move on much faster.
- I wasted my time, her time, and the efforts of many other people. Ultimately, in letting Mary go I think I did her a favor. I finally did what I had set out to do in the very beginning of the troubles: I trained her in who she was and the consequences it created.
- If actions, behaviors, and issues cannot be resolved

in a short period of time, then it is time to find someone else for the position.

- I needed to take care of the business and my clients before taking care of Mary. I tried to grow someone who did not want to grow. I did not want to face the reality and my business suffered.

Applying the lessons learned to your company:

- We cannot rely on a person based on resume and by checking references. The proof lies in the actions of the employee. If you see that there is a mismatch between what is on paper and the reality of the situation, have a conversation immediately. Include specific actions and behaviors that need to be changed.
- It is hard to say to someone, "It is not working." If you have made an honest effort at behaviors and issues that need to be resolved and there is no improvement, you need to find another person for that position.
- When you are the leader you should take input, but ultimately the direction of the company is up to you. If someone is trying to take it in a direction that is harmful for clients and growth, you must stop that person immediately.

39.

I FIRED A FRIEND

Marissa Levin
Information Experts

When I started Information Experts eleven years ago I did not separate friendship from business relationship. This changed quickly after an experience with my friend Joan (name changed). Joan had done projects for companies we both knew. From what I could tell, her work was excellent and she completed projects on time. A project came up that I knew Joan would be perfect for, so I hired her.

Everyone who works on projects with our company signs a non-compete clause, which states that he or she will not solicit or accept additional work from the client for a period of one year. Joan signed the agreement as part of her contract employment. After the project was completed, the client, who did not know about the non-compete agreement, asked Joan to do another project. She said yes. Joan did not say anything about the non-compete agreement and began doing the work.

Joan made two mistakes: She did not think that I would find out about her working on another project for the client, and figured if I did somehow know, I would not do anything about it because of our friendship.

Joan made two mistakes: She did not think that I would find out about her working on another project for the client, and figured if I did somehow know, I would not do anything about it because of our friendship. She was wrong in both cases. I did find out about the project and sent a certified letter to the client with a copy of her executed non-compete agreement. The client called me and apologized. He terminated her work immediately. I also sued Joan and got an injunction against her working for this client.

As a result, Joan lost the income from our client and all potential for future work with Information Experts. It was an expensive lesson for her to learn. Unfortunately the friendship was also gone. It was a casualty of the business.

What I learned:

- Joan greatly underestimated me and was counting on our friendship. She did not realize that our business transaction trumped our friendship.
- If I had done nothing when Joan worked directly for our client, the non-compete agreements that all of our subcontractors sign would become invalid in the future. I had to enforce the agreement.
- Friendship and business do not mix well. I had to learn to look outside friendships for subcontractors and employees.

- Eleven years later we have zero-percent attrition rate. Our employees did not leave. Even though I am not a friend of them, I always am tuned in to their personal lives. I try to be aware of what's going on and what is driving them. They know what is expected from the business relationship and what I provide as an owner. I have worked hard at being consistent and providing leadership.

Applying the lessons learned to your company:

- You must separate friends from business relationships. You must put the same regulations in place for friends that you would for any employee, subcontractor, or client. You must set the roles, responsibilities, parameters, expectations, deliverables, and other requirements/consequences in writing. This cannot be overlooked. Even though you are friends, one person is providing a service or product for another person's business. It is a professional transaction.

- Your employees are looking to you for strength, leadership, and consistency. They are not looking to you for friendship. As a business owner, it can get lonely. You need to find peers in other businesses for friends.

- If someone breaks the rules you must take action immediately, even if it hurts a friendship. You must show all the employees that you will enforce contracts no matter who the guilty party is.

40.

MY BOSS TOOK CARE OF ME IN A PERSONAL CRISIS
Nancy Slater
Seavest Realty

I work for a great couple, Paul and Pam Krug. This husband-and-wife team owns a real estate property management company, Seavest. I began at Seavest about nine years ago as a part-time employee. I have since become the operations and marketing manager with signature authority on checking accounts.

About six years ago, my adult son was killed in an automobile accident. I flew to his city to handle the arrangements. I called Pam and told her that I would not be coming in that day and explained what had happened. She assured me that I should spend the time taking care of my personal needs.

After the funeral I returned to town and appeared in the office. It was only a few days after my son was killed. I thought that it would be better to be there. Pam asked me, "What are you doing here?" I said, "I don't have any vacation or sick days and cannot afford to be home." She said, "Go home. The work will be here when you get back. You need to take care of yourself." I realized that I was definitely appreciated by Paul and Pam. Their understanding and care really helped in my crisis situation;

Their understanding and care really helped in my crisis situation; they gave me the time I needed to grieve and restore my mental health.

they gave me the time I needed to grieve and restore my mental health. I did not have to worry about keeping a roof over my head or food on the table while I was out of the office.

I am incredibly lucky to be working for such compassionate, great people, and I have learned so many things from them.

What I learned:

- Make mistakes. I have never been yelled at. Paul or Pam will explain that "this was wrong and we would prefer that you don't do this again." In addition, they hate surprises and will not tolerate a hidden mistake. Pam and Paul realize that we are human, but they expect us to be honest about, and correct and learn from, our mistakes.
- Family issues need to remain at home. I have never seen them talk about family issues in the office, and they have certainly never yelled at each other about personal things. The office discussions are about office issues.
- If you cannot be a cheerleader for the company you work for, you need to find another job. You are not doing anyone any good by gossiping or backstabbing.

- Know your employees. Each has a different personality and style and you have to manage accordingly. You cannot expect someone who does not like change to be excited about a new method of doing things. Do not criticize their reaction to the change. It will take some time for that person to get used to the new way of doing things.
- Test people. Give them a little responsibility and see what happens. If they handle it well, give more.

Applying the lessons learned to your company:

- Hire all four major personality styles. This ensures that you have a diverse work group with different ways of looking at the same problem. Ask for input. Each person's perspective will be different. You will find better solutions this way.
- Create a professional place to work. If you treat your employees well they will treat your customers well.
- When you explain things the first time your employees might not get it exactly right. Have the patience to help.

41.

I WENT FROM CORPORATE TO CLEANER
Kermit Engh
Fashion Cleaners/Omaha Lace Laundry

I bought my first company, Fashion Cleaners, fourteen years ago. I came from a corporate background and had no experience in the dry cleaning industry. To my surprise, the employees had never gotten together and talked; their ideas and suggestions for improving the business had never been solicited, and it took months for me to get them to open up. I constantly asked them to let me know what I could do to help them do their jobs easier and faster. At first they would just mention little things, like replacing the chalkboard with a whiteboard and markers, because it was cleaner. When they saw that I took these small suggestions, the floodgates opened and our meetings quickly became complaint sessions. That was not productive, so from then on, whenever there was a complaint, a solution had to be offered as well.

> *The culture at work became one of measurement, computers, and doing jobs quickly and efficiently.*

The culture at work became one of measurement, computers, and doing jobs quickly and efficiently. We had a dashboard for the week's production where we measured payroll, production, claims, and much more. Feedback was critically important. Everyone knew where he stood all the time and what was required to advance. Fashion Cleaners expanded to three stores, two routes, and forty-five employees.

In late 1999, I purchased Omaha Lace Laundry, which had four locations and thirty employees. The year 2000 was one of the toughest years I experienced trying to integrate the two cultures. Fashion Cleaners had computers, bar coding, efficiency, and teams working together; Omaha Lace Laundry had one computer, a calculator on the counter, and handwritten tickets. Their employees worked at a different pace. They stretched the work to fill the day or rushed through the work to make it. I had to bring them into the twentieth century.

I made the decision that during the integration no one would lose his position, but it was still hard on everyone. Many of the employees belonging to both companies switched locations. Many of the Omaha Lace Laundry personnel felt inferior to the other employees and said so even though they were never treated any differently. Whenever they brought this up, I pointed out that there was absolutely no benefit to the company for treating them badly. Obviously, they saw the logic in that response.

There were a lot of picnics, group hugs, and department meetings trying to integrate the two companies, get everyone to know each other, and feel like a cohesive group. The question "What things in the company are inhibiting you from doing your job?" was asked constantly. This was a cause-and-effect discussion and resolved a lot of issues between departments.

Two things really helped. The first thing that I did was to purchase the book *Who Moved My Cheese?* by Spencer Johnson for all the managers and supervisors. We read it and discussed it. I made everyone write down which character in the book they thought they most resembled, then we went around the table and revealed our answers to the group. Some of the people had vastly different perceptions of themselves than their co-workers had of them. It opened up a lot of people's minds.

Second, we became a client of Michael Gerber's "E-Myth group." We put in systems, provided clarity, and benchmarks. It forced us to provide continuous feedback to the employees and let them know how they were doing.

Although the year I bought Omaha Lace was the most difficult in my career in managing people, the effort and results have been successful. We are profitable, each employee contributes and knows how important they are to the organization, and we continue to come up with new ideas to better serve our customers.

What I learned:

- By creating the "no firing policy" during the merger I tried to salvage people that I knew were not working out. I should have fired them rather than let them cause disruptions. However, it was not my intention to clean house.

- People pay attention to what is important to their supervisor. If you measure and care about their efficiency and effectiveness, they too will. They want to know what it takes to succeed in your company.

Applying the lessons learned to your company:

- If you have a few people who are not on board with where the company is going, they do not need to be in your company. They will cause problems.
- Change is difficult for most people. There is a lot of mistrust at first. You need to be consistent with your message and actions. Then, people will start to test you; passing these tests and proving yourself dedicated and loyal will eventually lead to trust.
- Hire slowly and fire fast.

42.

FROM "US" TO "THEM"

Ellen Rohr

Owner, BareBones Biz

I had about one hundred jobs before I started my business, many of which were in the restaurant industry. I have done just about everything from dishwashing to shucking oysters to managing. I always worked hard and got along well with my fellow employees. We complained together and laughed about management's rules, policies, and usually, their lack of competency. It was "Us" against "Them."

One day the restaurant owner came to me and said, "Ellen, you have been doing a great job. Steve (name changed) is going into rehab. We would like you to replace him as manager. Are you interested?" I immediately answered, "I will do it."

> *But the biggest thing I did not realize was that my co-workers were not my friends anymore.*

I was handed the keys to the restaurant, and at that moment I went from being one of "Us" to being one of "Them."

I told myself that I had gotten a promotion. I forgot that there was going to be less money from tips, more hours, more responsibility, and more stress. But the biggest thing I did not realize was that my co-workers were not my friends anymore.

I walked out of the manager's office and the bartender asked me whether I had seen Steve because it was time to open the bar. I said, "I have the keys. I will open the cabinet for you."

The bartender just looked at me in surprise. Then his whole demeanor changed. He realized that I was no longer one of "Us." From this moment on I was no longer a friend who would laugh when he dropped a rack of glasses. He would have to be cautious and edit what he said in front of me. I had crossed the line. I was now one of "Them."

Since that day I have always been one of "Them." I learned to deal with the wall that separates management from employees and to become friendly, but not friends. Initially it helped to be an "Us" because it helped me recognize the dumb things that bosses can do to the people who report to them. I vowed never to be one of those incompetent managers that I had worked for as an "Us."

What I learned:

- Managers should always communicate. If you expect someone to follow your lead you need to let that person know where you are going. It is critical to explain what your goals, behaviors, and expectations are to an employee. Otherwise you may be going down one path and they will be going down another.
- Let people do their jobs. Why hire people if you are

going to do everything yourself? I found that you put yourself at risk every time you jump in and take over. The employee would not learn. Or worse, would not do the job, because he knows that you are always there to bail him out.

- Keep the same standards for yourself as you do for your employees. You cannot ask your employees to do something that you do not do. For example, I once wrote up an employee who did not make it into work on time on a day that I was twenty minutes late. What a double standard! I never did that again.

- Support your employees. They are on the front lines dealing with your customers. Sometimes they will make the wrong decisions, but as long as the lines of communication are open you can fix the problem.

- A quote from Abraham Lincoln that I love: "It's surprising how much you can accomplish if you don't care who gets the credit."

Applying the lessons learned to your company:

- As the manager you are responsible for setting goals. There should be a form of measurement or list of requirements in place for each goal so that the employee knows how to achieve it.

- You have the right to dictate what behaviors you will and will not tolerate. For example, anyone who lies, cheats, or steals should be fired.

• Your employees are your company to your customer. Customers do not see you; only the result of your management style.

43.

ESTABLISH DIVERSITY RELATIONSHIPS BEFORE YOU HAVE A CRISIS
Joe Schneider

In the late 1960s our shipping company decided to expand our business into the southeastern U.S. The company was renting space and beginning to hire employees, starting in Mississippi. Company policy was to hire based on the percentage of the population—if there were 25 percent minority in the area, 25 percent of our employees had to be minorities. I spent a week knocking on doors in Mississippi, trying to start relationships that would help us accomplish our equal employment goals. The local chamber of commerce did not help—they wanted two different buildings for the employees based on race. (This was the 1960s in the South—racial problems were still rampant). Two separate buildings were unacceptable to our company and I had to find a way to make the integration work.

Our company accomplished the goal: we hired to the percentage of the population, and everyone worked together in the same building. This helped establish trust and understanding within the community. We became a good corporate citizen in the eyes of the community, as well as a successful company. As a result, the relationships that we started fifty years ago are still in existence today.

This taught me a valuable lesson: Relationships are critical, and a company program that maturely deals with diversity issues is the best way to establish good, fair relations quickly. Our company established such a program after learning this lesson during our southeast expansion. The company sent twenty to twenty-five managers to inner city areas around the United States that they had never experienced before. Our purpose was to have them live, eat, and breathe in the inner city. They found out first hand what it is like to try

> *Relationships are critical, and a company program that maturely deals with diversity issues is the best way to establish good, fair relations quickly.*

to exist as a homeless person reliant on soup kitchens; how people survive without a roof over their head and a bed to sleep in each night; what the needs of these populations were. The company wanted these coddled, well-off managers to get a taste of the lives of the less fortunate.

It worked. When these managers got back to their jobs, they had a much better understanding of how to work with people from different cultures. As a result, they become better managers of our diverse workforce.

Having established such strong relationships with a wide variety of people helped me solve a number of problems, but one incident in particular comes to mind. One of our districts had twenty-five Equal Employment Opportunity Commission (EEOC) charges filed against it, charges that were ignored for three to four years. The local management had not done anything to build relationships and it was obvious through the complaints. It became critical. The company got bad press and we could no longer ignore what was going on. I got phoned in to help.

I knew the director of the EEOC, so I called him and he agreed to work with us. In addition, our lawyer in this district had worked for the EEOC and had a good relationship with them. Both these relationships worked heavily in our favor. We did not have to take time to build trust; it was already there.

Our company and the EEOC worked out a solution to handle these twenty-five charges. Our company and the EEOC assigned one person each with the authority to settle all the cases. As a result, all the cases were resolved within three months.

Did it cost the company some dollars? Yes. However, that money was far less than what it might have cost if more charges were filed or they continued to be ignored.

What I learned:

- Whenever a new district manager is promoted, I insist that the manager meet with the local area representatives for the EEOC, DOT, OSHA, and union. This person needs to build a relationship with the heads of these organizations.
- Teaching people about diversity works. It helps build trust between all areas of our company.
- Relationships between people are the key to a company's success.

Applying the lessons learned to your company:

- Training takes time and can be costly. However, good relationships and understanding among all employees is critical to business success.
- Encourage managers to build relationships with vendors, the government, and others. If there is trust rather than suspicion you will have a better chance of resolving a crisis quickly and with minimal damage to the company's pocketbook and reputation.

44.

MENTORS HELPED ME SUCCEED
Carnela Renee Hill

When I was interviewed for my job at AT&T I told my interviewer I was not going to be in that technical position very long—my goal was to be a manager and the entry-level position was just the beginning. I explained that I wanted a mentor to coach me and help me grow. My first day on the job I told my boss the same thing. He told me he would do everything he could to help me achieve my goals.

> *My mentors became my eyes and ears—whenever an assignment came up they thought I could do, they assigned the job to me.*

I was assigned to a team of eight people. Our manager traveled a lot and soon I was considered the acting supervisor. Whenever a problem occurred during my manager's absence, I handled and resolved the issue. Since my manager was gone more than he was in the office, many of the customer and HR issues fell on me. I handled all of them with the company and the customer in mind.

My actions were noticed by upper management and I soon had their ear. They assigned me a mentor and I found another one on my own. My mentors became my eyes and ears—whenever an assignment came up they thought I could do, they assigned the job to me. The higher-ups learned to count on me to get the job done right and within budget.

I was moved around so I could learn different functions of the company and different management skills. During one of the moves I had a boss who was jealous of my success. He felt that I name-dropped and was bothered by the fact that I had a great business relationship with many of the managers and executives in the business unit. This boss disliked the fact that special projects were requested of me by upper management.

AT&T was good to me. While working on my Executive MBA, they gave me every other Friday off for school. This boss could not believe that I could handle the added projects assigned by the executives, go to school, and perform the job responsibilities for my regular work. However, I did them successfully time and time again.

I soon realized that my jealous boss was trying to hold me back. However, when it suited his advantage, he used me. When senior executives said to him, "We need your senior person," I was that person. I always came through and made him look good.

As miserable as I was, the mentor relationships I had fostered got me moving forward again. They helped me realize that this boss was not going to be my boss forever and advised me to take whatever positive I could from the situation. Shortly thereafter, I accepted an advanced position as a district manager.

What I learned:

- I have always been a go-getter and completed the tasks that I was given with little to no direction, successfully and within budget. This trait got noticed and helped me achieve what I wanted to achieve. My success today is based upon God first, great mentors, and coaches next.
- Mentors definitely affected my career. They taught me that even in a bad situation, I had to turn it around and use it to my advantage. Bad situations do not last forever.
- Since I have had great mentors, I have become a mentor to others. I have shared what I have been taught. It gives me great pleasure to help others along the path to success.
- Always keep in touch with your mentors even if it is on an occasional basis. You never know when you can help each other again.

Applying the lessons learned to your company:

- Surround yourself with people who have a positive attitude and work to achieve something in life. Watch how they react and how people react to them. Always know where you want to go and see who can help you get there. You cannot do it alone. *If they do not help you initially, you have established a relationship and you will be rewarded and remembered later.*

- Success depends on you. Surround yourself with people who are successful.
- As a mentee you should help your mentor too. Ask how you can help and do what your mentor suggests. Do not make it a one-way relationship. That will cause the relationship to fail.

45.

I HAD A ROTTEN BOSS
Anonymous

I can now look back and laugh at this situation, though, believe me, it was not funny at that time. However, it did teach me how never to manage. My boss, John (name changed), purchased six flower shops and asked me to manage one of them. John's plan was to start with a small core of shops and gradually open more of them. However, he did not know anything about running a flower shop.

I kept the costs lower than the requirements but never saw a bonus; John had the bookkeeper tweak the reports so the shop never appeared profitable.

As I had the experience in the area, I was promised a percentage of the net profit of the shop if I kept payroll costs at a certain percentage, cost of sales at a certain percentage and so on. I kept the costs lower than the requirements but never saw a bonus; John had the bookkeeper tweak the reports so the shop never appeared profitable. I was furious, but the incident that finally made me leave happened on a Valentine's Day.

In the floral business, Valentines Day is usually the busiest day of the year. Now, John had a rule that anyone calling after 2:00 p.m. would get the flowers delivered the next day. We were abiding by that rule when one of John's buddies called at 3:00 p.m., wanting flowers delivered to his wife. I explained that I was sorry but we could not do it because all the delivery trucks were gone. If he would like to come in to the shop we could handle his request. He declined and hung up.

At the end of the day, I was very proud of my staff. We had generated over $10,000 in revenue and all the orders were delivered on time to our customers. We left the shop tired but feeling good about what we had accomplished. The next day, instead of congratulating us for taking care of our customers and the great revenues we had generated that day, John screamed at me in front of my staff for not taking care of his buddy's flower request. I was shocked that he was ignoring his own rule. Obviously, he wanted to blame us rather than explaining his rules to his friend.

My staff was horrified; they were very dedicated to me. We spoke after he left and I apologized to them. I explained that I was the buffer and the criticism needed to go through me. However, that incident sealed their opinion of his inability to manage. I left soon after this incident, and of the six flower shops that John originally bought, two were sold and four closed, including the one I had managed.

What I learned:

- Praise in public and punish in private. As the manager (and, therefore, buffer) I knew that I had to take the criticism, but John's tirade should not have been made in front of my staff. He undermined the morale and could not gain back the trust that he lost during this incident.
- John did not understand retail. When I managed the flower shop we always promised 85 percent and delivered 100 percent.
- You must follow through on promises. I was frustrated each month because I did not see a bonus. Later, I knew that the numbers were manipulated because I was keeping the costs under John's requirements.
- Ask the people in the trenches their opinions. In all of the managers meetings I attended, John never asked for our input. We knew what worked and

what did not, but he never asked. If he had, then the flower shops might still be open today.

Applying the lessons learned to your company:

- Your employees know what is going on. Ask for their opinions. They have a good sense of what will be profitable, and, as the manager, you should make the final decision only after gathering as many facts as you can. Communicate your decisions.
- Do not break your own rules for a friend. If you are going to break the rules, you need to explain to your employees why you are doing it and whether the rule is being abandoned or just ignored. Employees will not respect your decisions if you change the rules all the time for favored people.
- Trust is hard to gain and is easily lost. When you do something that makes your manager look bad in front of his or her employees, you will lose the trust of all. No one wants to be treated badly or embarrassed in front of others, and yelling rarely solves any problem. Resolving issues requires calm, rational discussions.

46.

SEXUAL HARASSMENT WAS ACCEPTED
Anonymous

I was the head of human resources for the North American division of a European company. This division was generating millions of dollars using high-paid talent. The vice president of sales and marketing, an American, was the genius behind bringing in the millions of dollars. He had hired a woman and taught her a lot, and they became friends. In fact, he showered attention on her, including sexual attention and heavy innuendos.

> *They considered it "sport," and seeking office romances was a generally accepted mode of behavior if kept quiet and under the covers (so to speak).*

According to her, he was the best boss that she had ever had. When she filed the complaint with me, she said that she trusted me to take it as far as it would go and that she wanted him controlled, not fired. He was brilliant and she did not want to ruin his career or his marriage. And, she still wanted to work for him. However, she wanted the sexual issues stopped.

To my surprise, the culture of this European company was totally different than the accepted business culture in the United States. This European company had managers in many cities and almost all European countries. Having affairs was common and nothing out of the ordinary. They considered it "sport," and seeking office romances was a generally accepted mode of behavior if kept quiet and under the covers (so to speak).

As a result of this discovery, I knew that the Europeans would not back me because they did not understand the laws of the United States. Even though my European boss was female, she had no clue how to handle this situation.

I carefully and confidentially brought the vice president in and told him that a sexual harassment complaint had been made against him. Ironically, he suspected someone else rather of making the complaint! I told him that it may or may not be that person and that I could not reveal who it was. Fortunately, he trusted me to do the right thing, and the shock of the situation woke him up. It was a turning point in his life. He stopped the harassment and the foul language. I knew his behavior changed because I made sure to pay attention to what he was doing. I did not want him to ruin his life and the lives of others.

Since the behavior stopped the complaint never went any further than the permanent notation in his file, which remains in my desk to this day. Neither family ever found out and both marriages remain strong. Eventually, the European company was sold and this division was absorbed into another company.

What I learned:

- What is accepted behavior in other countries may not be accepted in the United States, nor should these behaviors be emulated by U.S. executives. Even though I had no backing from my bosses in Europe I had to abide by what was legal in our country.
- Trust is an issue. The woman knew me and knew that I would deal with the situation fairly. She knew that I would protect her and do the right thing.
- Sometimes people want to get their point across without hurting the person they are complaining about. In this case, it could have ruined the career of a brilliant person. I had to deal with the situation privately and keep the trust of both. No one else could know what was going on. Keeping many secrets in my career was critical to me advancing.

Applying the lessons learned to your company:

- If someone files a sexual harassment charge find out why the charge is being made and the outcome that the person filing the charge expects. If it is for revenge and the person does not want to work for the company any more, you need to evaluate the truth of the story. You need to know the motive behind the filing as well as having the documentation that it has occurred.

- Sexual harassment charges are serious and must be investigated. A good attorney can help here. Make sure that you have one who is familiar with sexual harassment claims.

47.

I DIDN'T WANT TO BELIEVE
Rod Toner
CFM Equipment Distributors, Inc.

As a sales manager, it is my responsibility to assemble a skilled, outside sales team known as "territory managers" in our industry. Recruiting for these positions takes a considerable amount of effort, strategy, and creativity. Once a qualified candidate is located, my company required that a Caliper assessment exam be administered. The intention of the assessment is to match the personality traits, skill sets, and integrity of the candidate against the profile of the job position.

One of the positions I recently filled was in a very high socioeconomic area of our territory. Our company prefers that our sales personnel live in their territories. Due to the high cost-of-living area to be addressed, I had difficulty locating interested applicants who lived there. As patience is not one of my virtues, I became frustrated after a couple of months over my lack of progress. I decided that I needed to think "outside the box." Maybe I could convince somebody *not* initially interested in the job to become interested, and then actually take the job!

The question then became, what am I looking for in a territory manager for that particular territory?

The opportunity in that territory was huge and untapped. A person with many relationships in the industry would be the person I needed. A strong technical person with excellent product knowledge would be a plus. And a person with high integrity and good work ethic is always important to elevating our company's reputation in the market.

Well, as fate would have it, I knew a person who exactly fit this profile. My candidate was a job-site supervisor for a struggling contracting firm. He needed a change of scenery and I convinced him that he had all the prerequisites for the job. Per company policy, he

I was so pleased with my resourcefulness and good fortune to have found my man that I ignored the warning signs.

took the Caliper assessment. I was not overly concerned when my recruit's assessment profile came back covered with red flags. He passed the integrity portion with flying colors, which was critical to me, so I ignored the rest of the report that suggested he might not be the right person for the job.

I was so pleased with my resourcefulness and good fortune to have found my man that I ignored the warning signs. Unfortunately the assessment exam knew a lot more about my candidate's worthiness to succeed as a territory manager than I did. His style of communication, lack of flexibility and lack of self-starting ability were challenges for him—exactly what the assessment predicted.

The customers tested him. He could not talk to people all that well, which hurt his sales. Within a few months I had a time-consuming situation on my hands. I had to have a pep talk and rally him everyday to confront difficult customers and develop potential customers. He got depressed and resigned within six months. Today he is once again managing projects and is much happier.

What I learned:

- When hiring a new employee, the applicant needs to take the initiative to seek the job. I will never again try to convince somebody to accept employment they are uncertain about.
- While the Caliper assessment exam is supposed to only represent one-third of the selection process, I will never blatantly disregard the results again.
- Despite his lack of progress I did not want to fire him because I did not want to admit I was wrong. Firing him probably would have been the best thing for him—I let him be miserably unhappy for six months.

Applying the lessons learned to your company:

- Assessments can be a good tool to aid in the hiring process. Most are fairly inexpensive and can help you avoid making a hiring mistake. However, the entire decision should never be made solely on the results of the tool that you choose.
- If someone is not working out and is obviously not happy, the best thing for you to do as a manager is to let him go. You can do this humanely by being honest and direct with him as well as giving him time to find a position that he will be happy with.

48.

WE TURN TEENAGERS AROUND
Ellen Frederick, Manager
Burger King, Duluth, Georgia

[Note: Ellen asked me to change the names of the teenagers.] I have been managing restaurants for more than forty years. For the past five years I have been the manager for the Burger King restaurant in Duluth, Georgia. We have consistently been in the top 10 percent of all Burger King restaurants in the United States. We are proud that Burger King always brings executives to our store because they can count on the fact that we were doing things the right way.

In the past five years turnover has been minimal overall and non-existent in my kitchen staff. Most of the turnover is through advancement. I have lost some great employees to promotions within the Burger King system. I hire mainly teenagers. Many have been in trouble. I start them as cashiers and give them the opportunity to advance.

This is the story of two of my latest teenagers: Steve and George. Steve came to me at seventeen. He had recently lost his father, which sent him into a tailspin. He had quit high school and was floundering.

George has a wife, a child, and a drug conviction. He also had dreadlocks when I met him. I told him to cut his hair and come back to talk with me. He came back with his hair short so I knew that he was serious.

I always try to look at the good in people. However, I am no pushover. Everyone in the store knows that we

I have lost some great employees to promotions within the Burger King system.

do things the Burger King way, per the operations manual. Everyone knows that we talk with and get to know our customers. The only deviation I made from the regulation was that I put the cashiers in a shirt and tie. I know that if Steve and George look good, they feel good.

Everyone is cross-trained. If we need help taking orders, people in the back can help. If we need help cooking, people who normally take orders pitch in. This takes more training time but is worth it. There is no one in the store who is too good or would not do a job that needs to be done. Steve and George were indoctrinated into this philosophy. They quickly learned what was expected of them. In addition, I always explained why we were doing certain things and how their careers could advance when they mastered different tasks.

Steve and George quickly mastered their cash drawers. I knew then that these bright men would not be happy as cashiers for the rest of their lives. So, I started training them to be shift supervisors. I explained that if they mastered the shift supervisor position, they could advance to an assistant manager, then manager. Steve also had to get his General Educational Development (GED).

As part of the training, they were responsible for making the schedules. George screwed up the schedule in the computer and I did not fix it. He realized his mistake when the wrong work team showed up one day. He asked me why I did not fix it. I told him that he had to be responsible for his actions and that he had to make it right. (Of course, I had a back up plan, just in case.) This was a great learning lesson for him!

I made them take practice tests. I drilled them about answering interview questions. I made sure they understood, had practiced, and could articulate what the next job would entail. They were prepared to advance.

Steve got his GED and passed all of the Burger King

tests to become an assistant manager at the age of seventeen. He was motivated. However, Burger King said that he was too young. When he turned eighteen they relented and Steve became an assistant manager. It also looks as if at nineteen he will be a general manager for a franchise store. I take pleasure in knowing that he has the training, communications skills, and knowledge to do a great job in his store.

George has passed his tests and is an assistant manager under me. He is looking to advance to manager, and it is only a matter of time until he achieves this goal.

What I learned:

- Taking teenagers and turning them around takes time and tough love. It has given me great pleasure and satisfaction. A teenager can thrive if he knows what is expected of him, what happens if he makes a mistake, and what the rules are.
- Unless the mistake will cause a great deal of harm, do not fix it. Let the trainee find it, correct it, and learn from it. Always have a backup plan ready, just in case the trainee does not see it.
- Cross-training is essential. It ensures that everyone can help out in a pinch.
- Teaching these teenagers helps them become productive adults. They learn to communicate with customers, a skill critical for an adult and transferable to any career.

Applying the lessons learned to your company:

- Management is all about communications. Be clear about expectations and the rewards and consequences of positive and negative behavior.
- Follow the manual. Create one for your company if you are not a franchisee. The manual should state the requirements for each position, how to do that job, and how to advance to the next position. This lets you know that things are done correctly in your absence.

49.

OUR FRANCHISEES DIDN'T BELIEVE I COULD BE AN EFFECTIVE CEO

Dina Dwyer-Owens

The Dwyer Group

My father, Don, started our franchising business. He was grooming Robert Tunmire, who he found to be excellent at driving sales and building the franchises. I was being groomed in the real estate side of the business and my sister, Debbie, was being groomed to handle operations.

During the transition process, my father died unexpectedly. At that time we were a public company and it was decided that Robert was the best person to take the role of president and CEO as he had the best knowledge of franchising. He had a tough job overcoming my father's legacy and in addition, he had to put up with my sister and me, two very strong women. But those were not the only challenges Robert would face over the next five years. His real focus was to get the company back to its core franchise concepts in trade services and

> *There was a lack of confidence in my abilities that I had to confront before it got out of hand.*

trim the fat of other concepts that did not fit our overall picture. In the meantime, sales suffered without Robert's sole attention. By 1998 the board decided to replace Robert with me as acting president and CEO. Robert became executive vice president of the company and went back into the role of building franchise sales.

This was a tough thing for Robert to swallow, although I sensed that there was some relief on his part to get back to doing what he does best. I was hoping to prove I was the best person for my new position. But many of the franchisees did not know me and questioned if I was the right person to run the group. There was a strong group of Mr. Rooter franchisees in the Northwest, and one of them decided to do a straw poll and ask whether I should be CEO. The answer was no. There was a lack of confidence in my abilities that I had to confront before it got out of hand.

I called the Mr. Rooter franchisee who initiated the

straw poll. I told him that I was surprised that he had done this. I explained that I knew that he did not know me well, but I asked him for his support anyway. I agreed that I did not know much about the nuts and bolts of the plumbing and electrical business. However, I knew the customer and what the customers wanted. I understood their needs. I asked for six months. I told him that if I could not do it I would be the first to admit it and step aside. He agreed and gave me a chance.

The franchisees watched closely. In six months I proved my ability to run The Dwyer Group and earned their support. None of this would have been possible without the help of my talented executive team.

Once the franchisees realized that I could do the job and their franchises and businesses were not in trouble there were no more straw polls. In fact, the initiator of the straw poll has become one of my greatest supporters.

What I learned:

- Faith in yourself will help you do the right thing and solve issues.
- When negative situations arise, find out what is true and acknowledge the facts. Find out what they need to know that might change how they look at the issues.
- Make the tough calls and do what you need to do to get the issues resolved before they become crises. Ask for what you need and do what you promise.

- A great team around you can help you move mountains.

Applying the lessons learned to your company:

- When customers or your team show a lack of faith in your abilities get rid of your emotional reaction and look at the facts. Study what is really going on, and what are the incorrect perceptions of it? You must show them the reality.
- You have to make the tough calls and ask for a chance to make things right. Most people will give you that chance with a reasonable timeline.

50.

EMPLOYEES LIVING THEIR DREAM
Mike Nelson
Orlando National Bank

I was brought in two years ago to turn around Orlando National Bank. It was losing money, among other problems. I got the board's commitment that the solution I was proposing was a long-term solution. We did not want to just temporarily fix the bank and sell it for a quick profit in three to five years. Everyone wanted a bank that we could be proud of and to hold our heads high in the community.

I believe that my leadership and management role is twofold: (1) to create a framework for the long-term vision and (2) create an environment where individuals in the bank have the opportunity to help refine the vision, add to it, and own a piece of it. We knew that the only way that we were going to be effective was to develop employees. My overall role was to help them become all they intended to be. Here are two examples: A lady in her fifties had been a teller for about eighteen years when I joined the bank. She was intimidated when I came in to meet everyone. It was obvious she was not comfortable. I found out that she was a good teller even though she was timid and rather reserved. Two-and-a-half years later, she is now speaking on behalf of the bank on women's issues. She goes to networking groups and sells the bank.

Another example is a gentleman who was a branch manager for a number of years. Unbeknownst to me, he was an accounting major in college. He really wanted to understand the operations side of the bank and account for dollars at the end of the day. I agreed even though he had been doing a good job as manager and was leaving a position I would have to fill. He is now on the operations side of the bank, much happier and much more successful.

I asked my managers, "What do you really want to do?" and they were required to ask the same question of those who reported to them.

I tried my best to give our employees the tools to help connect them with what they really wanted to do. I asked my managers, "What do you really want to do?" and they were required to ask the same question of those who reported to them. Most people could not answer this at first. Some had never been asked. We created open dialogs and tried to find connections in the bank for where people wanted to be. One of my senior vice presidents wants my job. I have got to find a way to prepare her.

We knew that the bank would grow stagnant and continue to have problems if the management of the bank stayed totally reliant on the structure that was in place. I had to be interested in the people, not the structure. I had to find out where each person truly fit with what their dreams were and help each develop the tools and skills necessary to achieve that dream. We knew that we had to help them get there or that person eventually would become dissatisfied and leave.

Were there some people who left the bank? Absolutely. They found out their dream was not in banking or doing the job that they had. In the long term, this was better both for the bank and that person.

As a result of putting people in positions they truly want, we have been able to do some unique and wonderful things for our community. We have had many initiatives including the Women's Initiative, where we make a demonstrable difference in our customers' lives. Most of our employees are not on commission. We make it clear that their job results and their on-going employment is dependent on helping our customers achieve the financial outcomes they want. In addition, our mayor has asked us to be on the Women's Business Initiative for our community. Overall, our people fiercely defend the bank. Most tellers do not go to networking events and pitch their bank. Ours do.

Our profitability starts with our employees performing jobs they love and contributing to the customers' lives positively.

At the end of the day, the bottom line is whether the bank is profitable or not. In the past two-and-a-half years the bank has become more and more profitable with an ever-increasing bottom line. Our profitability starts with our employees performing jobs they love and contributing to the customers' lives positively.

What I learned:

- People and profits are not mutually exclusive. You need to have people in the positions that they want to be in and working with an understanding that their job is to profitably take care of their customers.
- You cannot be afraid of moving people around. If someone is not happy, that is not good for them or the customers. Eventually they will leave and you will have to replace them; why not find a place

where they can utilize their talents to the fullest before they leave the company altogether?

Applying the lessons learned to your company:

- By asking the simple but tough question, "What do you really want to do?" and supporting the answer, you will have better employees and a better working environment for all; even if some people decide that they are better off not working with your company.
- Do not be afraid to put people where they really want to be. You will find that they will often shine.
- Bottom line profitability is the result that matters. Without a profit the organization would not exist, even with great people. Everyone must understand how they contribute to the profitability of your organization and they need to always keep that in mind.

PART TWO

WHAT YOU CAN DO
ABOUT IT

CHAPTER TWO

SEVENTEEN CRITICAL SURVIVAL STRATEGIES

The fifty stories shared in the previous chapter describe many of the management situations that you are likely to encounter. The responses to these situations can be distilled into seventeen critical survival strategies. If you are having problems with one of your employees, these strategies can help you resolve them.

1. Know the Outcome You Want from the Resolution of a Conflict with an Employee.

What is the best possible solution? The answer to this question may be difficult and definitely should not be arrived at when you are angry, frustrated, or in any emotional state. You must be rational in your thinking. Sometimes you will need to talk with others before taking a decision. Once you have the desired outcome in mind, determine what it is going to take to get there.

If intelligent employees are consistently underperforming, it may be best to let them go through a career readjustment program. This program helps a person find a job that suits his or her talents. Most of the time, the program will result in the person no longer working for you. At other times, a bright, intelligent employee makes a dumb decision or does something stupid that is completely out of character. In these cases, you must immediately help those people realize the error they made, ensure that they learn from the mistake, and get a promise from them that it will never happen again.

Finally, there are instances where your employee policy manual dictates the outcome of a specific situation, so you have no option other than following the company's requirements. This may not result in the outcome you desired, but you must always follow company procedure.

2. Create a Team of Mentors.

Find people who are capable of helping and willing to help you succeed. Mentors watch out for your interests because you have shared your goals with them. They will call you when they come across a customer or a project that is right for you. And if they see you doing something stupid, they will tell you about it. You might have different mentors for personal and business issues. You might have mentors who help you through one project or who guide you for years. They can be personal associates or trusted business advisors.

Mentors can be found everywhere. They could be at your same level or above you in your company. They could be at another company. Or they may be business owners or managers outside your company with years of experience.

You can and should call on your team of mentors when you have ideas for them or when facing a management crisis. Get their input, and the group may pool their experience to come up with a great solution that helps everyone achieve their goals. In this case, you are acting as both boss of and mentor to your team.

3. Communicate.

Everyone who reports to you needs to understand what their role is and what your expectations are. Here's why: if one person is standing on each of the four corners of an intersection and there is a car accident in the middle, each person will see it differently and their conclusion about the accident will be different.

The same is true for management. If you want a certain result, you have to communicate clearly the result you expect. Then you have to ask for feedback to ensure that everyone understands what is expected of them. Otherwise, different team members will have different viewpoints on what you said and their results will be not be exactly what you wanted, because the team based their performance on their unique viewpoints rather than yours.

Do not expect your employees to read your mind. They need clear direction from you as to what they should be doing and need feedback as projects or tasks progress. Without communication, each of your team members may proceed in a different direction, and as a result, nothing gets done the way you want it.

4. Confront the Bad Issues Immediately.

Bad situations never go away. They only get worse. It is imperative that you talk, at the earliest, with the person who offended someone or did something wrong. The worst thing you can do is to say nothing. Employees may not realize that they did something wrong, or if they are testing your tolerance and you do not say something, then they think they got away with it and the bad behavior is likely to be reinforced.

Of course, it is tougher to have a negative discussion than a positive one, but you need to handle problems as quickly as you handle good things. Make sure that the employee knows that if something was done wrong, it needs to be corrected, and it cannot happen again. Some employees watch managers handle the problem. A manager will either gain or lose respect depending upon how the employees perceive the manager's actions. Also, if you do not say something immediately and just wait for that person's review, he or she is likely to be shocked. They will think, "Why didn't you tell me earlier? I could have fixed the issue."

Follow the employee manual when negative situations occur. If someone is not doing his job, commits a fireable offense, or does something wrong, follow the actions outlined in the manual. If you do not follow policy, people will not respect the company rules and will start to abuse your leniency. If you do not enforce the rules, then there are no rules and you have anarchy.

5. You Do Not Have to Be Nice. You Have to Be Fair. As a manager, you have to make tough decisions. The best working environments are ones in which employees know that they are treated fairly, what is expected of them, and what will happen if they do not follow the rules. You cannot enforce the rules for some of your employees and choose not to enforce the rules for others. If you do so, those who are favored will know it and potentially take advantage of it. Those that are out of favor will know it too and feel that they are getting unfair treatment. This could destroy their morale and lead to expensive legal bills.

You cannot play favorites. There may be times when you hate enforcing the rules because you really like an employee who screwed up. However, you cannot have different rules for employees whom you like more or who are more productive than others or whom you perceive to be so valuable that you cannot lose them. The first time you let someone get away with breaking the rules and not being disciplined, you have lost that policy. Others will think they can break those rules, and they can. Favoritism has gotten a lot of companies into legal trouble and cost them thousands of dollars.

The rules can change over time. As your business grows or as the legal environment changes, sometimes policies must change to conform to new business conditions. If someone challenges you in court, ignorance of the law is no defense. So, be sure to keep abreast of the employment laws in your state.

When you have to make those tough, unpleasant decisions, make sure everyone knows that you did not enjoy making that decision and that everyone is equally involved in the process. Demonstrate a sense of fairness, so that people will not feel singled out and will accept the changes more rapidly.

6. Be Clear about Evaluation Criteria.

Performance appraisals are a fact of life. As a manager, make sure that you understand what criteria you use to evaluate performance. As an employee, understand the actions you are being evaluated on. The evaluation criteria should be in writing and signed off by both the boss and the employee before the employee even begins working. If there are changes or additional projects that you are asked to take on, find out whether they affect the performance appraisal. Get it all in writing.

Likewise, communicate the performance criteria for your employees in writing. These criteria should be reviewed quarterly and updated. There should be no surprises at a performance review.

What if you own a business? Your performance appraisal is a combination of your bottom line, your employee retention rate, and your customer retention rate. If your company is profitable with a low turnover rate, then your performance is acceptable. In addition, your advisory board will help you keep on track the goals you set.

7. Have a Sexual Harassment Policy and Follow It.

This is absolutely critical. You will also need ongoing training on dealing with issues relating to sexual harassment. There are very many stories of women and men being harassed by their bosses or their subordinates. Unfortunately, many are not reported and the people just quit, and you are left wondering why you lost a good employee. Most of the time, the departing employee sees no other way out and does not want to deal with the situation any longer.

There are other times when an employee unfairly accuses a manager of sexual harassment. In such cases, report the issue immediately and have a notarized statement of the event.

Robin Bond, Esq., deals with sexual harassment issues as part of her legal practice. According to Robin, the best line of defense is to have a good policy, ongoing training, and implementation of that policy if need arises.

8. Hire People Who Are Smarter than You Are.

Smart people will help you succeed. They can make you look good. The key is to establish the objectives and let them do their jobs without micromanaging them. Do not be jealous. Do not hold them back; listen to their ideas. They might know more than you do.

9. Encourage Disagreements, Discussions, and Debates.

The phrase "two heads are better than one" is very true. It is wiser to have many people working on a problem than trying to solve it by yourself. The most successful meetings are ones in which open debate is encouraged. However, mean words are not allowed. The goal is to solve an issue. Many times the first idea is not the best and the right solution comes as a result of debate.

Having confidence in your abilities helps encourage debates—just because an employee has the best idea, it does not invalidate your own skills. As the manager, the final decision is up to you, but be willing to admit that your initial idea was not the best one. During discussions and debates, be open to finding a better solution. Go with the best solution even if it was not your idea. If you do not, you may find yourself out of a job.

10. Praise in Public. Punish in Private.

People like positive attention, and if your employees see it being bestowed on others, it could spur them on to the same good performance. On the other hand, people are embarrassed by punishment when it is meted out in front of others. If you have to discuss negative issues during a meeting, do not single out the person or people who committed the mistake. It is likely that everyone knows beforehand who they are and that the guilty party is already embarrassed. Approach it as a problem to be solved—describe what happened, then ask what can be done to ensure that it never happens again. If you encourage open discussion and debate, you will probably get some creative solutions.

Even if a meeting has to deal with negative situations, unless everyone committed the mistake, do not imply that everyone did. Always end a meeting on a positive note. This is critical, so that employees are in a good frame of mind when they leave the meeting and get back to their work.

11. Know How to Manage Different Personality Styles. Learn how best to communicate with your employees. Different people react differently to discussions; some you can be very direct with, while others require more tact. Some will take it personally; others will realize that you are not attacking him but his behavior on the job. With some employees, you can raise your voice because some may not respond otherwise. Some will accept change quickly. Some like the status quo.

Personality profiles can help you match a person to a specific job. There are many personality profiles that you can use to help as a hiring tool. They foster group communication and tolerance. Many a times, these profiles help build esprit de corps with team members. When team members complete the profile, they tend to have a better understanding of how they communicate and why other people on their team communicate as they do. This leads to mutual understanding and less friction at work.

12. Take a Calculated Risk.

Sometimes the most successful manager is the one willing to try something contrary to common belief. It takes confidence in your team to step out of the norm, and this enhances the ability to fight for what you and your team believe. At the same time, when you or a team member makes a mistake, admit it and take responsibility for it as the manager or team leader.

Risk taking is part of management. "No decision" is a decision. A "no decision" will often frustrate your employees and have them lose respect for you. Do your homework and trust your gut. It is usually right.

13. Keep Family and Business Separate.

This applies to every company, from large corporations to family-owned businesses. Managers must be aware of employees bringing personal issues to work. If a normally productive employee becomes nonproductive for no obvious reason, usually the reason is a family issue. Talk it over with him and, if need be, give the person time off to deal with it. Explain that you need him to be productive and focused when he is at work, but that you understand that he is going through a rough patch and may need some time.

In family-owned businesses, owners and managers have to make hard decisions when a family member thinks a job is his birthright and does not perform productively. It is also difficult to make succession decisions. Tension can build if issues are not resolved. This is seen in *Dad Couldn't Make a Decision* Once the major stumbling block between Dad's second wife and his younger children was resolved, the process could go forward.

If nonfamily members come across family issues superseding work, they are likely to feel resentful and good employees may leave. This occurs in *I Instituted an Anti-Nepotism Policy*. Family issues can affect performance. It is best to separate them as much as possible.

14. Follow the Employee Policy Manual.

Every company should have a policy manual which describes acceptable and unacceptable behavior as well as consequences for not following policy. It should include the guiding principles of how you expect your employees to behave on the job and the rules for inappropriate behavior. The good and bad about employee manuals is that once the rules are put down on paper, everyone has to follow them, even if it hurts! Favored employees must be disciplined as per the same rules as someone who is not a favored employee. Otherwise, the company can get into legal trouble for not following the rules equally for everyone.

All employee manuals are different. Some states require certain important elements to be incorporated. Therefore be sure to have it reviewed by a labor lawyer, even though it may cost some money—better to be safe than to feel sorry. And in the long run, it could save you a lot of money.

Employee manuals usually begin with a letter from the president welcoming the new employee to the company. The letter contains, at the minimum, the company's philosophy of management, how it expects the employee to take care of customers and to interact with fellow employees, and the quality of work expected from them. It is usually a page long and sets the tone for the document.

After the welcome letter, the manual should touch on these topics:

1. *Customer service*. Point out that customers write the employees' paychecks.
2. *Quality*. State that employees must strive to do their jobs right the first time. If an employee is not sure of what is expected of him, he should ask the manager. There is no such thing as "a dumb question."
3. *Admitting mistakes*. The company's honesty policy is stated here.
4 *Job security*. Write that continued employment depends on growth and profitability.

5. *Employee at will.* Even after the probationary period, the employee is not a "permanent employee" and can leave at any time or be terminated at any time in some states.

6. *Nominal working hours.* Describe the usual working hours for the company. Then state the exceptions.

7. *Overtime and training.* State the policy for paying for training and overtime. This may vary depending on whether the employee is a field or office employee.

8. *Probationary period.* The typical probationary period is ninety days. At the end of the ninety days, the employee is an employee at will.

9. *Emergencies.* What to do if an accident, sickness, or a personal emergency arises. Advise the employee whom to call and within what time frame.

10. *Normal pay day.* Explain time card/time sheet policies and when checks are issued.

11. *Performance evaluation.* Describe the criteria for performance evaluations. Put a copy of the performance evaluation in the employee manual so that employees can see exactly what is on the form.

12. *Immediately fireable offenses.* Describe actions that may cause immediate termination of employment. Typical actions include use of illegal drugs/alcohol or being under the influence of them while on the job, stealing, falsifying time records, refusing to comply with instructions from your supervisor, use of abusive language, and sexual harassment.

13. *Disciplinary action.* This is usually some form of the "three strikes and you're out" rule. Present copies of the forms in the employee manual.

14. *Drug-free workplace.* Each state has different rules on drug testing, noncompliance, and so on. The details regarding a person being subjected to a drug test within twenty-four hours of an accident are given here. The company's workman's compensation insurance carrier may have a few words to be inserted here. The drug policy may be printed here or in an appendix.

15. *Alcohol.* Explain the rules related to alcohol consumption in the workplace.

16. *Sexual harassment.* Describe, at the minimum, the reporting rules, implementation, and training.

17. *Confidentiality.* The employee is not to release confidential information about customers or other employees to anyone. Explain the consequences of releasing confidential information.

18. *Dress code.* Explain how the company expects employees to dress on the job.

19. *Vehicle.* If an employee is driving a company vehicle, then there are certain rules that he must follow. These usually include policy on using company vehicle for personal use, maintenance, cleaning, allowable drivers, and actions to be taken if the employee meets with an accident.

20. *Company telephone and computer.* Explain the

business and personal use of these communication devices. If an employee is responsible for paying for any personal use, state how the company is repaid.

21. *Holiday.* State the holidays that the company pays for, when an employee is eligible for holiday pay, and what happens when the holiday falls on a Sunday.

22. *Sick day.* If the company pays for sick days, the number of sick days and how they are paid is explained here.

23. *Bonus.* If the company pays bonuses, explain who is eligible, how the bonuses are determined, and when they are paid.

24. *Vacation.* Explain how vacations are paid and the length of service required for each vacation increase.

25. *Jury duty and military policy.* Describe how employees will be paid while on jury duty or military leave.

26. *Death in the family.* Define immediate family bereavement pay.

27. *Worker's compensation.* This policy and actions are usually mandated by the state. Get information from your worker's compensation insurance company to print here.

28. *Health insurance.* It should mention when the employee is eligible for health insurance and what the employee must do to enroll in the plan.

29. *Retirement benefits.* If the company has a 401(K), simplified employee pension (SEP) plan, or other

retirement plans, explain the eligibility requirements, how to enroll, and how the plan is administered.

30. *Safety policy.* State how employees are expected to act in a safe manner on the job and what to do if they observe unsafe conditions. There should also be a statement regarding compliance with Occupational Safety and Health Administration (OSHA) policies.

31. *Equal opportunity employer statement.*

At the end of the policy manual, include the following page to be signed and placed in the employee's personnel file:

I have read these policies and procedures manual, including the drug and alcohol policy, and agree to govern my actions in accordance with the instruction given herein.

_____   _____

Name   Date

I have witnessed the signature of the employee named above.

_____   _____

Supervisor   Date

15. Never Fire Anyone When You Are Mad.

Anger is an emotional state. You cannot think rationally when you are emotional. If your gut reaction and emotion says to fire a person, wait until you calm down before taking any action. A cool head leads to logical thought, and that is when you should make any big decision.

16. Fire with "Ruthless Compassion."

If you have to fire someone, do it professionally and with "ruthless compassion."

Ruthless: No matter what the employee does—argues, cries, screams, yells, complains—he is fired! Many will tell you he is your best employee.

Compassion: He is to be fired in the nicest possible manner in a private location.

Firing and laying off people are unfortunate facts of life for owners and managers. It is an unpleasant but necessary part of job, so do it with ruthless compassion. And if at all possible, if you have a talented employee who is just not suited for the job she is in, try and recommend a career path that may be better suited to her skills.

17. Say Thank You.

You are successful when your team members are successful. Say thank you and sincerely appreciate the hard work they do. They are your support structure without whom you could not survive. Saying thank you is one of the easiest and most appreciated actions you can perform. Managers usually say more to a team member who made a mistake than they do to someone who performed a task well—humans tend to remember the negative far longer than the positive. Good deeds go untold and unremembered, while everyone knows about mistakes. Take the time to say "thank you" for your employees' accomplishments. And make a note of the accomplishment in his personnel file. When it is review time, you will see both the positives and the negatives.

There are many quick and easy ways to say "thank you": a pleasant comment while you are passing an employee in the hall; a note in a paycheck; a letter to a spouse; a memo to his/her boss (with a copy to the employee) outlining the good work that an employee performed. None of these takes a lot of time, and all produce great benefits.

CHAPTER THREE

SIX STEPS TO SUCCESSFULLY GROOM YOUR NEXT MANAGER

Grooming a manager is a long-term process with no guarantee of the results. The person that you think will be your next manager may not want to be a manager, or he may try the position, decide that he does not like it, and leave. Or something completely unconnected could happen—like his wife or significant other getting a promotion in another city. On the other hand, you might unexpectedly find someone who can step up to the position, take on the responsibility, and shine.

When choosing the next manager, do not limit yourself to those who are already managing. You might find field personnel or nonmanagement office personnel who are longing to become a manager. I have known many people who tried to make the management transition and could not, while others shone as managers even though they were average or slightly below average nonmanagers. The skills to be a manager are different from the skills required by nonmanagers. Keep an open mind with respect to who you start grooming to be the next manager.

Here are six steps to successfully grooming your next manager.

Step 1: Decide How Much Information He Needs.

- The first thing all managers must have is a scorecard. How will he be evaluated? Will it be on the financial results of his department? Increased sales? Increased productivity? Decreased expenses? Some other measurement tool? He needs to know when his team is doing well and also where the problems are so they can be corrected. These goals and measurement tools must be communicated by the new manager to everyone on his team.
- To have an accurate scorecard, what information does he need? Decide what is confidential and what can be shared. If he gets access to the financial statements of his department, he must learn how to read them. This is usually a challenge for a new manager. However, this problem can be quickly overcome by taking the right financial or accounting classes.
- What financial data are you willing to share with

employees? Some companies keep all financial information secret from all employees. The employees have no clue as to how they earn profits for the company. Many of the employees in these companies feel that the company and its top personnel are earning a lot more than they actually are.

- Other companies share financial data with their employees. The owners and financial managers teach them about profits, how they are derived, and why they are important for the company's survival. These employees know the profitability of their jobs and the profitability of the company overall. They understand how they impact profitability. They do not know the exact details with respect to everyone's salaries and other overhead expenses, but do have an appreciation of how they contribute to the bottom line. In these types of companies, when profitability problems arise, the employees often come up with ways to solve them. Many times bonuses are calculated on productivity. Jack Stack's book *The Great Game of Business* is a classic example of how this sharing works.

- You, as an owner or manager, must decide how much information to share with the employees and how much information to share with the new manager. The manager must understand that you trust him with confidential information about his department and the company. He must learn how to give accurate but broad information to his team without revealing the details.

- The best way to start training is to hold, at a minimum, monthly review meetings with the new manager. At this meeting, discuss the measurement requirements for each team member and how successful each member has been in achieving the goals. Depending on your company's policy, you might also discuss financial information. For the first few months you will have to lead the discussion. After that, the new manager should lead the discussion. If the new manager is trusted with the entire company's financial statement, the manager should report on the financial condition of his department in relation to the company. He should point out any problems he sees and tell you what actions he is taking.

- The team members and the manager will be evaluated on reaching the department goals. Make sure the new manager has the right information so he can succeed.

Step 2: Introduce the New Manager to His Team.

Introduce the new manager to his team in a group meeting. Before this meeting, have a discussion with the new manager and tell him to prepare a statement for the meeting. The talk should be brief and express the fact that he is looking forward to working with the team and helping everyone achieve their goals. He should stress that he is there to lead and help where necessary.

- If this is a promotion from within, then an introduction to the background of the new manager is not necessary. If the new manager is meeting his team for the first time, open the meeting with a discussion of his experience, accomplishments, and what he will be doing. Express confidence in the new manager and then have him give his speech.
- The meeting should be short, and give everyone an opportunity to ask questions. There might be some hard ones concerning past events or intricate company policies that the experienced manager should answer. However, do not monopolize the conversation—it needs to be the new manager's meeting. You are just there for support.

Step 3: Responsibility, Authority, and Accountability.

Managers need the responsibility to do the job, the authority to do what is necessary to get the job done, and the accountability (rewards or consequences) for the results.

- It is much easier to give the responsibility and accountability than the authority. As a manager, sometimes it is difficult to oversee the process and resist the urge to do the work yourself. If you do not agree with his way of doing things because it is not how you would have done it, discuss your concerns privately with the manager. If you jump in and over-rule him, you will undermine his authority.

- Here is an example: Suppose you have a new manager who is responsible for building product sales. Talk with him and get his agreement on a goal of increasing that product's sales by *X* percentage (or dollar figure) by *Y* date. Make the goal very clear. Have him give you ideas on how he will motivate his team to accomplish the goal. You might also give him some suggestions, but make it clear that the decisions are his. He has the authority, responsibility, and accountability to get the job done. He must understand and agree to the consequences if he does not reach the goal. Make it clear that you are available for questions and help, but not to do his job.

- If a team member comes to you trying to overturn a decision made by the new manager, you must tell that person that you stand behind the manager's decision. You cannot overturn his decision even if you disagree with it. Talk with the manager privately and get his reasoning. If you mutually come to a different solution, he must be the one to implement it.

- Your job is to manage the process. This means that you watch and make suggestions only when asked for them. The only time you should offer an idea is if you see a blatant error that will harm the department or the company. If you do see a blatant error, speak with the manager privately and explain to him how what he is doing could be a major mistake. Have him give you suggestions for correcting it, and if you agree with his suggestions, tell him to carry out those corrections.

- When a new manager is doing something that you may not have done, but is not an incorrect action, staying out of it may be one of the most difficult things for you to do. But you *cannot* interfere. The manager may not do things exactly as you might do them, but he will get them done. As long as he produces the desired results morally, legally, and ethically, and the customers are happy, everyone wins.

Step 4: Hard Lessons to Learn.

Here are some things you should teach a new manager:

1. You cannot be friends with the employees who work for you. This is probably the toughest lesson to learn. Teach the new manager that he has to be friendly, but cannot be friends with his team. Explain that he has to retain his objectivity. Managers who have been promoted from within a company sometimes have to find whole new groups of friends, which can be very lonely at first.

2. Bad news does not go away. People do not like to deal with difficult problems; they hope ignoring it will make it go away. A new manager must learn that he has to deal with problems immediately. If he

ignores them, they usually get worse. Teach him to attack the tough issues as they surface. He is now in a position of power, which means he is accountable for the performances of those he manages. He has to learn to confront the issues quickly and resolve them.

3. Treat everyone on your team fairly. A manager has to do things that are fair for everyone. Some people will like his actions and some will not, but what is important is that the decisions are good for the group and the company. A manager cannot make a decision that will favor one person over another. For example, if a good employee demands a raise and threatens to quit if he does not get one, many times it is better to let that person quit. If he gets a raise, everyone will know that they can threaten to quit if they want a raise. This is not the environment a manager wants.

4. Discipline with fairness. You cannot let one person get away with doing something that is against the rules, and then punish other employees for doing the same thing. Everyone has to play by the same rules, and the same punishment should be doled out for the same crime, regardless of who perpetrated it.

5. Return telephone calls. If you have an unhappy customer, deal with him immediately. If you recognize the caller's name and know that one of your team members is working with that customer, speak with the team member first to get her impression about

why the caller is unhappy. Letting messages sit only makes an unhappy customer even unhappier—try to return telephone calls and resolve problems within 24 hours. After all, customers write your paychecks.

6. You have to make hard and unpopular decisions. Managers and owners get the privilege of seeing the whole picture, and if things are not going well, it is their job to fix it. If that means no overtime, shorter hours, layoffs, and so on, managers must be the ones to make and implement those choices. If it means firing someone who is not doing his job, they are responsible for that as well.

7. Maintain objectivity. Sometimes maintaining objectivity is difficult to practice with people you worked closely with before you were promoted to manager. If you have been working side by side with a colleague, you know his weaknesses. Can you deal with those weaknesses and mistakes objectively? Maybe, as his colleague and friend, you helped cover for his gaffes. Now that you are his boss, can you deal with those mistakes and discipline appropriately?

Step 5: Hiring.

Managers must become skilled at hiring—the better you are at hiring, the less likely you will have to fire an employee. Before you hire, first specifically define the details of the job. What will the new employee be doing? What skill levels are required? What is the pay range? What type of advancement is possible? How much in additional revenue or decreased expenses do you have to generate to justify the position?

- Answer these questions even if you are replacing someone who left the company. What are the real reasons that employee left? If an employee left because he felt overworked, underappreciated, and there were not enough hours in the day to complete his job duties without constant overtime, then closely look at the job description. You might find the job demands to be unreasonable and need to change them.

- When you are grooming a manager and it is time to hire an additional employee, make the manager justify the need for the new position. Once the need is sufficiently established, conduct practice interviews with that manager. Review the standard list of questions and make sure that he knows what he can and cannot ask (no race, religion, family, sexual preferences, medical history, etc.). Make sure that he asks open-ended questions, which require more than a yes/no answer. Role-play with him so that he is comfortable when he conducts the real interview.

- After the interview, the new manager must check the applicant's references and have a discussion with you. The new manager should make his case for hiring a person if he thinks the person is a good fit.

Remind him that if he hires the person and that person does not work out, he has the responsibility for firing that person. This is a task that nobody likes.

Step 6: Firing.

Firing people is never pleasant. However, it is part of management, something a new manager needs to be aware of and will sometimes have to do. Even after being in business for more than 25 years, I hate firing people. Laying off employees is just as difficult as firing them, sometimes even harder. Since it is done because of cash flow and through no fault of the people being laid off, it can be hard to justify putting them out of a job.

There are generally two types of firing: the "three strikes and you're out" and for committing the "immediately fireable offenses." If you have a "three strikes and you're out" rule for inappropriate behavior or incompetence, then the new manager must have someone in the room to verify the verbal and written warnings. The manager should give ways the person can improve and time limit by which the improvements must be made. These should be put in writing after the discussion and signed by the manager, the person being disciplined, and the witness. By the time the third strike comes, firing should be no surprise to anyone, including the person being fired. In addition, when a new manager fires someone, there should be two other people in the room.

It takes time as well as the right combination of personality and attitude to groom a new manager. There are no guarantees of success. However, if you find the right person, he will create a good working environment for his team, which will increase productivity and profit, which, in turn, will make you look good. Delegate and check his progress, rather than doing the work yourself. Concentrate on your own responsibilities and have faith in those you have chosen to mind the details.

CHAPTER FOUR

THE SEVEN GREATEST MANAGEMENT MYTHS

From my experience, my research, and the stories that managers shared with me, I have arrived at this master list of the greatest myths about management. If you have made any of these mistakes, hopefully you have learned the painful lessons that accompany them and will not make them again. If you have not made these mistakes, don't! Avoiding them will keep you on the path to success.

Myth 1: Your Employees Can Read Your Mind.

You expect your employees to know what you want them to do. Unfortunately, they cannot read your mind. You get frustrated, angry, and upset when they do not do what you expect them to, but they cannot instinctively know what you want. You must communicate your desires clearly.

- If you see an employee doing something wrong, it is your job to let him know and to correct it. Many a times, the employee has no clue that he is doing something the wrong way, and unless it is pointed out, he may never know. The fact that you know does no good unless you spell it out.
- Communicate. Be verbal. Compliment the positive and correct the negative. Explain the goals of the organization and develop each team member's goals and actions to help develop the company.

Myth 2: You Can Be Friends with Your Employees.

Never. You can and should be friendly, but you cannot be friends. You have power over them because you are evaluating their performance. If you treat them like friends, they will not respect you, and if they do not respect you, you will be an ineffectual leader. Managing can be lonely, especially when you were promoted from within. You have to develop a totally new set of friends at work.

Myth 3: Your Employees Have the Same Agenda as You Do.

Your employees are not you—they do not have your goals and desires. This can cause conflict, especially when their goals are totally different from the goals you have been given as a manager. You could subconsciously hold back team members who are more ambitious than you are. This could cause frustration and resentment.

- Find out what your team members' goals are, so that you can help them get where they want to go. Of course, they have to be productive members of your team no matter what, but that does not mean that they cannot be developed for further advancement if they can handle doing both.

Myth 4: Your Employees Have the Same Work Ethic as You Do.

They do not. You may be willing to put in the long hours to advance, and your team members may not. You may live to work. They may work to live.

- This myth is especially true for small business owners. You think your employees are willing to work as hard as you do, receive as little pay as you receive. Your employees do not have the same passion for the business as you have. They are looking at it as a job, not as life.

- Accept the fact that your employees may not work as hard as you do. However, are they working hard enough to justify their pay? Are they productive? If the answer to these two questions is yes, accept the fact that your employees are not willing to put in the long hours and do not hold it against them.

- Another way to look at this myth is with your employees' actions. Are they moral and ethical? Are they cutthroat? Are they willing to lie to get ahead? Your employee policy manual should have policies for appropriate behavior. If a team member is not willing to comply with or violates one of these policies, he must be disciplined, even if he is the most productive member of the team.

Myth 5: You Can Change People.

Unless you impact an employee when he is a child you cannot change his values. How he grew up has a great impact on how he behaves and his actions as an adult.

- Research shows that by the time a child reaches the age of eighteen, his values are locked in. In fact, most values are formed by the time a child is ten and are merely refined in the teenage years.
- Trying to change people will result in frustration and futility. They may change for a short time, but unless there is a compelling reason for change or a significant emotional event that shocks them, people go back to their natural state. Find the people who have the behaviors you want and teach them the skills they need to be productive.

Myth 6: You Can Do It Alone.

You need people to help you achieve your goals. If you want to be successful, get raises, and get promoted, you need the help of the people who work with you. If you try to do everything, you will not get anything done. The best managers teach their team members what needs to be accomplished in order to be successful and then make sure they do it.

- Solicit ideas and suggestions from your employees; go into the field, have lunch where your employees have lunch (break room, cafeteria, etc.), sit with the receptionist, and just talk to them. Ask questions about their jobs, listen to their answers, and implement the suggestions. Your employees have great ideas on what to do and what can be improved; they generally do not tell you because most are not brave enough to offer suggestions when they are not solicited.

- The most successful companies I know meet with their employees to jointly set goals and rewards for reaching them. This is one way to motivate your employees.

Myth 7: Your Employees Are Irreplaceable.

The reality is that no one is irreplaceable, not even you. Your most productive employee could get hit by a truck on his way to work and be gone in an instant. What would happen if he were not there? Everyone, including you, leaves the company at some point. If you think employees are irreplaceable, then they have power over you and can get away with doing things that are counter-productive to your goals. They can ignore policies because they know they will not get fired. You will have chaos.

Avoiding these seven myths will help you be a better manager and help your employees respect you as manager.

WORDS OF WISDOM

The managers profiled in this book offered many words of wisdom to current and future managers in hope that their words will help others.

- Be willing to say, "I don't know." Accept the fact that others who have more experience can teach you. You get their respect as well as their knowledge by asking for their help.
- Have a sense of humor.
- Acknowledge what each member of your team contributes. Everyone is important and should understand how he or she fits in the company.
- When you are the supervisor, you are responsible for the team's performance. If there is a problem, it is your problem, not the individual's problem. When

speaking with management, you must accept the responsibility for the team and not blame anyone. Of course, you will deal privately with a team member who made the mistake.

- Document every incident related to age, sex, race, creed, and religion, no matter how small or insignificant it might seem. You do not know the motivation of that individual and might need the documentation later. The statements should be notarized, but not by a notary within your company; one who works for an attorney is better.

- Do not take too long to have a discussion after a negative incident. Action should be taken immediately to avoid the incident escalating into a major crisis and distracting everyone from work.

- Managing sales people takes the same skill set as raising kids. You have to be a nurturer, mentor, and coach to succeed.

- Acquire the necessary management skills as quickly as you can. If you need to, beg and plead for management training. If your company does not have a training program, find one elsewhere.

- Hiring family members is never a solution to the problem of not being able to meet your hiring goals, especially in a large, publicly traded company. In fact, it often proves to be the reason for falling short of your goals. Talent acquisition goals must always be tied to sound talent-retention strategies. Having a fair and unbiased leadership team for hiring and firing is critical.

- You have to do what is right. Talented people may leave the company because they feel they are not being treated fairly.

- Even in human resources, patience and salesmanship are needed skills. You have to be able to sell your ideas and beliefs to upper management as well as the employees on your level and those under you. You need patience to do what you know is right, especially when there is a lot of resistance.

- Your company is only as good as your employees. Keeping a positive work environment is critical to success. Try to treat everyone as family as much as possible. Know what is going on in their lives outside of work and how it might affect their performance.

- You, as the leader, set the tone. If you enjoy what you are doing, everyone on the team sees it and will have a more positive attitude. To be successful, you need everyone pulling in the same direction. Have everyone work with you rather than for you.

- By treating your employees with respect, your customers will get respect. If customers see a great team environment, they are more comfortable with you and are more likely to give you repeat business.

- Healthy discussions and disagreements are critical for success. If your team just rubber stamps your decisions without discussion and debate, you will not know what they really think. Your employees work in the trenches of the business; some of their ideas could be catalysts that might cause the group to move in a different, better direction.

- Find a mentor who can help you.
- When a crisis hits you, you must keep your composure and a level head. If you lose your cool, you will lose the ability to resolve the situation. You cannot think rationally when you are emotional.
- Find good advisors for your business. Their vantage point will let them see what you cannot as you are too invested in the company; make sure that they are willing to be open with you about the errors they see.
- Poor performers do not leave. You have to run them off. Good performers will leave on their own if what is expected of them is not clearly defined and if they are unsatisfied and confused.
- People want to follow great leaders. They want direction and discipline. The reality is that they are not happy when they can get away with things they know they should not be able to get away with.
- Communicate your expectations well. People need to understand how their work will be judged.
- Job duties and the tasks that an employee will be evaluated on should be in writing. Both parties should agree on expectations and requirements. When these change, amendments should be made to the job description so that there are no surprises during reviews.

- Managing employees is different from being on their level. Wanting everyone to be happy is a nice sentiment but impossible.

- If an employee threatens to quit in order to get what he wants, even if he is your most productive employee, let him quit. The first time you do not, you will have anarchy because others will figure out that they can threaten to quit to get what they want.

- Have a formal sexual harassment policy in place, and hold sexual harassment training classes on a regular basis. If the company has a policy in place, it immediately has an affirmative defense. If training is occurring on a regular basis, then there is a message that the company does not condone sexual harassment. Encourage people to report all incidents and assure them that the information will be kept confidential.

- Be sensitive to the self-esteem of the person you are going to terminate. Suggest a new career path and point him in a new direction, one in which you think he can succeed. Terminating an employee should be done with compassion. You want an amicable parting rather than a contentious one.

- Conflict-resolution strategies work whenever two people are not communicating, be it a corporate, nonprofit, or family disagreement.

- If you see a new manager who is having issues resolving conflicts, step in to help. The manager will appreciate it (and hopefully will learn from it), as do the rest of the team members.

- Even if you have a good employee who does good work, if he does not follow company policies, he must be fired.
- Succession planning is often difficult. Many a times, owners of family businesses want their children to assume the reigns of the business. They need to face the reality that their children may not want to or may not have the capability to lead the company.
- Have a list of questions that you ask every interviewee. This way you can compare the answers you receive and help ensure a fair evaluation of all your applicants.
- People want to be heard. Listen to what they say. This will help you manage their behavior more effectively, as you will know more about them as people.
- Competition between peers often brings the results that you want. Everyone will strive to be the best when they are all evaluated the same way.
- Make sure that your company manual is reviewed by an attorney familiar with employment law. The attorney will make sure that you do not get stuck with a rigid clause. It is worth the cost of the review.
- A new employee can cause resentment, especially if he is hired to improve a department. Make sure that you encourage other employees to learn from the new hire. Do not let resentment build up or it could destroy your department.

- The employees need a consistent message from the top. One manager cannot say one thing that is totally opposite from what another manager says. Mixed messages cause paralysis rather than productivity.

- You do not have to take shouting and inappropriate behavior from anyone. People can discuss things as rational adults. Whenever I am confronted with irrational, emotional behavior, I ask that person to return when he is calmer so that we can rationally discuss the issue.

- If the business does not fit with your morals and ethics, you do not belong there. You will be miserable and stressed out.

- Team environments are critical to success. When there is one winner and one loser all the time, people will stop helping other people. Then the company loses, the customer loses, and the employees also lose.

- Praise in public and punish in private.

- Your employees know what is going on. Ask for their opinions. They have a good sense of what will work and will not. As a manager, you should take their input and make the final decision after gathering as many facts as you can. Communicate your decisions.

- Trust is hard to gain and is easily lost. When you do something that makes your manager look bad in front of his employees, then you will lose the trust of the manager and his employees.

- People may not like the decisions you make. However,

most will accept them if you explain your reasoning and are honest. Acknowledge that you do not expect them to agree with you, but that you want them to at least understand your thinking. Be direct and give the bad news in person, even though it is hard to do. Do not hide behind a piece of paper.

- Separate friends from business relationships. You must put the same regulations in place for your friends that you would for any employee, subcontractor, or client. You must set the roles, responsibilities, parameters, expectations, deliverables, and other requirements/consequences in writing.
- Admit to your mistakes. Bosses hate surprises and most will not tolerate a hidden mistake; besides, ignoring it will probably only make it worse. Admit to your mistakes immediately, and learn from them.
- People pay attention to what is important to them. If you measure and care about their efficiency and effectiveness, they will also reciprocate. They expect to know what it takes to succeed in your company.
- Hire slowly and fire fast.
- Let people do their jobs. Why hire people if you are going to do everything yourself? You put yourself at risk every time you jump in and take over. The employee will not learn. Or worse, he will not do the job at all, because he knows you are always there to bail him out.
- You have to keep the same standards for yourself as

your employees. You cannot ask your employees to do something that you do not do.

- Surround yourself with people who have a positive attitude and work to achieve something in life. Watch how they react and how people react to them. Always know where you want to go and see who can help you get there. You cannot do it alone.

- Assessments can be a good tool for aiding in the hiring process. Most are fairly inexpensive and can help you avoid making a hiring mistake. However, the entire decision should never be made solely on the results of the tool that you choose but on a combination of the applicants' résumé, proven work history, the tool of your choice, and your gut feeling.

- The key to management is listening and asking questions. The best way for a new manager to learn is by asking questions to experienced managers, who just listen and make the new manager discover the answers on his own.

- People and profits are not mutually exclusive. You need to have people in the positions that they want to be in and understanding that their job is to profitably take care of their customers.

- Bottom line profitability is the result that matters. Without profit, the organization will not exist, even with great people. Everyone must understand how he contributes to the profitability of the organization and should always keep it in mind.

ACKNOWLEDGMENTS

A very special thanks goes to each of the managers who shared his or her story with me. All were heartfelt, truthful, and sometimes painful to recall. I appreciate your candor and willingness to help others who will follow in your footsteps.

Next I thank Brenda Bethea, my assistant for more than sixteen years. She has watched the growth, the failures, the near misses, and the successes over the years. Until the writing of this book series, she had not transcribed dictation for a long time. I appreciate her nimble fingers, dedication, no-nonsense style, and support in this and other endeavors.

I have a wonderful group of people whom I work with at iBusinessChannel.com. Thank you for allowing for my crazy schedule and doing what needed to be done at a moment's notice because I forgot something while I was writing this book.

My team at Sourcebooks continues to be a great team. It is a joy and a pleasure to work with you. Peter Lynch, Tony Viardo, and all of you behind the scenes who help shape, promote, and get this book into the hands of managers who can benefit from it have my appreciation for the hard work you do.

My grandfather and my parents shaped my belief in continuous learning and sharing, so that others can learn from you. Thank you for the words of wisdom and, more important, for letting me make mistakes and learn from them over the years. Specifically to my mother who looks in *The New York Times* bestsellers list every Sunday: have some of the patience you taught me. This is a journey. You will eventually see my books there!

Thanks to my daughter, Kate. As a teenager you may be too young to appreciate some of the stories you proofread for me. Hopefully you will remember them and use them in your working career to be a great boss!

Finally, to my husband Bob, two loving, appreciative words: *Thank You!*

INDEX

A

Accountability, of managers, 217–19
Alcohol addiction, 92–95, 208
Anger, firing and, 211
Anti-nepotism policy, 31–35
Army lessons, 35–38
"Ask Them the Right Questions" (Whitecotton), 103–07
Assessments, 239
Authority, of managers, 217–19

B

Behavior, childish, 27–30
Bitzis, Charlie, 89–92
The Blair Witch Project, 75–79
Bonuses, in employee manuals, 209
Bosses, 170–73
Brindak, Paul, Hermine, Juliette, and Olivia, 135–38
Bullying, 127–31
Businesses, failure of, 1–2

C

Childish behavior, 27–30
Communication, 22–23, 49–52, 197–98, 234
Company policy, 110–13, 205–10, 236
Compassion, ruthless, 211

Compensation, 42–45
Competition, 107–10, 236
Compromising, 75–79
Computer, in employee manuals, 208–09
Confidentiality, in employee manuals, 208
Conflict, 89–92
Conflict resolution, 79–82, 235–36
Confrontation, 198–99
Construction, 42–45
Corporate boards, 49–52
Countries, behavior differences in, 174–77
Cowie, Robin, 75–79
Crisis management, 46–49, 153–55, 234
Cross-training, 180–84
Customer service, in employee manuals, 206

D
Death in family, in employee manuals, 209
Debates, 202
Decision making, 142–46
Disagreements, 202
Disciplinary action, in employee manuals, 208
Discussions, 202
Diversity, 163–66
Documentation, 16–20, 232
Dreams, employees and, 187–91
Dress code, in employee manuals, 208
Drug-free workplace, in employee manuals, 208

Dwyer-Owens, Dina, 184–87

E
Emergencies, in employee manuals, 207
Employee at will, in employee manuals, 207
Employee manual, 110–13, 205–10, 236
Employee performance, 52–55
Employees
  dreams and, 187–91
  fear of, 59–62
  irreplaceable, 229–30
  work ethics and, 227–28
"Employees Living Their Dream" (Nelson), 187–91
"Encouraging Competition Got Me Results" (Harlan), 107–10
Engh, Kermit, 156–59
Entrepreneurs, 96–99
Equal Opportunity Employer statement, in employee manuals, 210
"Establish Diversity Relationships Before You Have a Crisis" (Schneider), 163–66
Ethics, 131–34, 142–46, 237
Expectations, 55–59

F
Failure, admitting, 6
Fairness, 199–200, 220
Family

hiring, 232–33

vs. job, 124–27, 204–05

Family issues, 113–17

Fear, of employees, 59–62

"Finding My 'A' Employees Fast" (Humphries), 52–55

Fireable offenses, in employee manuals, 207

Firing, 211, 223–24, 235, 238

Franchises, 184–87

Frederick, Ellen, 180–84

Friendship, 150–52, 226, 238

"From 'Us' to 'Them'" (Rohr), 160–63

G

Galloway, Patti, 42–45

"Getting the Owner of a Family Business to Plan for Succession", 138–41

Global operations, 82–85

Grooming, of managers, 213–24

H

Harlan, Susan, 107–10

Health insurance, in employee manuals, 209

Hill, Carnela Renee, 167–70

Hiring, 221–23, 232–33, 238

"His Sales Masked the People Problem", 99–103

Holidays, in employee manuals, 209

"How I Managed a Global Operation" (Wells), 82–85

Humor, 231

Humphries, Joe, 52–55

I

"I Caught the Problem at Point Easy" (Weems), 79–82

"I Cursed at My Boss", 20–23

"I Didn't Know What My Bosses Wanted", 55–59

"I Didn't Want to Believe" (Toner), 177–80

"I Fired a Drunk", 92–95

"I Fired a Friend" (Levin), 150–52

"I Fired My Star Employee", 110–13

"I Had a Rotten Boss", 170–73

"I Hired the Wrong Person" (Nelson), 146–49

"I Inherited an Employee Who Hated Me", 120–23

"I Instituted an Anti-nepotism Policy", 31–35

"I Made the Tough Ethical Decision", 142–46

"I Managed Childish People" (Miller), 27–30

"I Manage Strong-Willed Entrepreneurs...And Listen to Them" (Ritter), 96–99

Immaturity, 27–30

Information, for managers, 214–16

Integration, 163–66

Intelligence, 202

"I Put My Family Ahead of My Job" (Quinn), 124–27

"I Taught Customer Service to Grunting Teenagers" (Winberg), 86–88

"I Was Afraid of My Employees", 59–62

"I Was Thrown into Management" (Strickland), 11–15

"I Went From Corporate to Cleaner" (Engh), 156–59

Izenberg, Illysa, 39–42

J
Job, vs. family, 124–27, 204–05
Job security, in employee manuals, 206
Jordan, Steve, 72–74
Jury duty, in employee manuals, 209

L
Levin, Marissa, 150–52
Listening, 96–99, 236, 239
Location, 99–103

M
Management
  myths about, 225–30
  reasons for, 5–8
Management styles, 117–20
Managers
  good vs. bad, 2
  grooming, 213–24
  introducing to team, 216–17
  teaching, 219–21
"Managing the Start Up of Our Family Brand"
  (Brindak), 135–38
"Managing Through a Crisis", 46–49
"Mediating Family Issues Made Me Sick" (Owen),
113–17

Mentors, 167–70, 196–97, 234

"Mentors Helped Me Succeed" (Hill), 167–70

Military policy, in employee manuals, 209

Miller, Mark, 27–30

Mistakes, in employee manuals, 206

"My Boss Didn't Operate in the Real World" (Izenberg), 39–42

"My Boss Took Care of Me in a Personal Crisis" (Slater), 153–55

"My Client Was Sexually Harassed By His Female Boss", 66–72

"My Direct Reports Were Fighting" (Bitzis), 89–92

"My Employee Was in the Wrong Job" (Jordan), 72–74

Myths, about management, 225–30

N

Nelson, Clay, 146–49

Nelson, Mike, 187–91

Nepotism, 31–35

Nonprofit boards, 49–52

O

Objectivity, 221

"Our Franchisees Didn't Believe I Could Be an Effective CEO" (Dwyer-Owens), 184–87

Outcomes, 195–96

Overtime, in employee manuals, 207

Owen, Norma, 113–17

P

Pay days, in employee manuals, 207
People, changing, 228
Performance, 72–74
Performance appraisals, 200–201, 207
Personal crisis, 153–55
Personality profiles, 203–04
Pets, 24–27
Praise, 202–03
"The President Tried to Bully Me", 127–31
Probationary period, in employee manuals, 207
Profitability, 239
Protection, 16–20
Punishment, 202–03

Q

Quality, in employee manuals, 206
Questions, 103–07, 236, 239
Quinn, Ralph, 124–27
Quitting, 235

R

Relationships, 163–66
Resentment, 236
Respect, 233
Responsibility, of managers, 217–19
"Retaining My Workers Was Tough", 63–66
Retirement benefits, in employee manuals, 209–10

Risk taking, 204

Ritter, Rick, 96–99

Rohr, Ellen, 160–63

Ruthless compassion, 211

S
Safety policy, in employee manuals, 210

Schneider, Joe, 163–66

Scorecard, for managers, 214

"Serving on Nonprofit Boards Was Hurting Me" (Stallings), 49–52

Sexual harassment, 16–20, 66–72, 174–77, 201, 208, 235

"Sexual Harassment Was Accepted", 174–77

Shouting, 127–31, 237

Sick days, in employee manuals, 209

Slater, Nancy, 153–55

Small Business Administration, 1

Solutions, 195–96

Stallings, Deborah, 49–52

Strategies, survival, 195–212

Strickland, Lea, 11–15

Succession planning, 138–41, 236

Survival strategies, 195–212

T
Taucher, Fred, 35–38

Teams, 11–15, 89–92, 231–32, 237

Teenagers, 86–88, 180–84
Telephone, in employee manuals, 208–09
Territory Managers, 177–80
Thank you (saying), 211–12
Threats, by employees, 59–62
Toner, Rod, 177–80
Training, in employee manuals, 207

V
Vacation, in employee manuals, 209
Vehicle, in employee manuals, 208

W
"We Bought a Company and Left Former Owners in
   Place", 117–20
"We Changed Our Compensation Plan" (Galloway),
   42–45
Weems, Susan, 79–82
"We Had to Find a Compromise" (Cowie), 75–79
Wells, George D., 82–85
"We Needed a Clear Pet Policy" (Woods), 24–27
"'We Need to Part Ways' Was Music to My Ears",
   131–34
"We Turn Teenagers Around" (Frederick), 180–84
"What the Army Taught Me About Management"
   (Taucher), 35–38
Whitecotton, Kathryn, 103–07
Winberg, Joanie, 86–88

Wisdom, words of, 231–39

"A Woman Sexually Harassed Me", 16–20

Woods, Richard, 24–27

Words of wisdom, 231–39

Work environment, 233

Worker's compensation, in employee manuals, 209

Work ethics, employees and, 227–28

Working hours, in employee manuals, 207

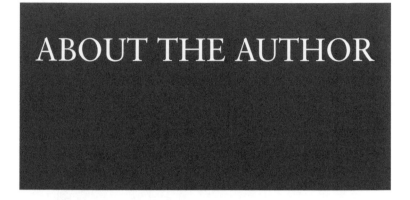

ABOUT THE AUTHOR

Ruth King is a seasoned entrepreneur. Over the past twenty-five years, she has owned seven businesses. Her first business, Business Ventures Corporation, began operations in 1981. Through Business Ventures Corporation, she travels throughout the United States, coaching, training, and helping businesses achieve the goals they set.

She has been involved with many different businesses over the years, with a wide range of interests, including Internet, television, music, video graphic production, healthy house products, and T-shirts. Ruth is passionate about helping adults learn photography and participate in marathon races. She helped start an adult literacy organization in 1986 that currently serves over one thousand adults per year. She ran the Boston Marathon in 2004 and 2005.

Ruth holds bachelor's and master's degrees in chemical engineering from Tufts University and the University of Pennsylvania, respectively. She also holds an MBA in finance from Georgia State University.

Ruth has spoken for national and state associations meetings, national and local trade shows, manufacturers, distributors, and others in forty-nine states. She is the author of *The Ugly Truth About Small Business*.

To share a story for the next *Ugly Truth about*™ book or to invite Ruth to speak, email her at: ruthking@iBusinessChannel.com.